DOING EDUCATIONAL
RESEARCH IN SCHOOLS

MB: For Claire, without whom, none of this would have happened.
RM: For Pamela and Owain who gave me the time, space and encouragement to complete this project.

DOING EDUCATIONAL RESEARCH IN SCHOOLS

MARK BETTENEY & ROBERT MORGAN

S Sage

3rd Floor, HYLO
103–105 Bunhill Row
London, EC1Y 8LZ

2455 Teller Road
Thousand Oaks,
California 91320

10th Floor, Emaar Capital Tower 2
MG Road, Sikanderpur, Sector 26
Gurugram, Haryana – 122002
India

8 Marina View Suite 43-053
Asia Square Tower 1
Singapore 018960

Library of Congress Control Number: 2025947601

British Library Cataloguing in Publication data

A catalogue record for this book is available from the British Library

Editor: James Clark
Editorial Assistant: Harry Dixon
Production editor: Sarah Sewell
Copyeditor: Raxshana Ravindraraj
Proofreader: Girish Sharma
Indexer: TNQ Tech Pvt. Ltd.
Cover design: Victoria Bridal
Typeset by: TNQ Tech Pvt. Ltd.
Printed in the UK by Bell & Bain Ltd, Glasgow
BB0363621

ISBN 978-1-0362-0900-1
ISBN 978-1-0362-0899-8 (pbk)

CONTENTS

ACKNOWLEDGEMENTS

This book is dedicated to the hundreds of students whose research projects we have supervised over many years. Their enthusiasm, interest and insight covering an impressively wide range of education topics have been the inspiration for this book. Their curiosity and determination repeatedly reminded us of the value of research work.

We are grateful to our university colleagues for their knowledge and assistance.

We also wish to thank, in advance, the teachers and mentors in schools who will continue to model the importance of research-informed practice.

ACKNOWLEDGEMENTS

ABOUT THE AUTHORS, AND SELECTED PUBLICATIONS

Dr Mark Betteney is an Associate Professor in Education, Language and Learning at University of Greenwich. He trained to be a teacher in 1988-9 and taught in primary schools in northwest Kent and southeast London until 2005. In that time, he led the teaching of music and literacy in three schools and became intrigued to know whether teaching children to read music in the early stages of language acquisition would benefit their ability to learn to decode text. The pursuit of this question resulted in his doctorate and in his ongoing interest in education research. He became a Senior Lecturer (teacher training) at London Metropolitan University in 2005, then a Principal Lecturer at University of Greenwich in 2010, and an Associate Professor in 2022.

Betteney, M. (2025). 'What do changes in policy regarding the teaching of phonics since 1995 disclose about successive UK education policymakers' understanding of early reading skills?', *Literacy*, 59(2), pp. 199–206.

Betteney, M. & Charlton, K. (2021). 'Music: Composing, performing, listening and structuring (all without fear)', in Gibson, P. & McDonald, R. (eds), *Inspiring Primary Learners*. London: Routledge, pp. 121–132.

Betteney, M. & Brooks, G. (2015). 'Can reading skills which are developed through the reading of music be transferred to benefit the early decoding of text?', *International Journal of Multidisciplinary and Comparative Studies*, 1(4), pp. 57–72.

Betteney, M. & Brooks, G. (2014). 'Learning to read text and learning to read music: Conceptual and pedagogical parallels', *International Journal of Multidisciplinary and Comparative Studies*, 1(1), pp. 6–16.

Dr Robert Morgan is an Associate Professor in Primary Education at University of Greenwich. He trained to be a Primary Teacher in 1993-94 and taught in primary schools in Torfaen and southeast London until 2007. He currently teaches on undergraduate and postgraduate teacher training programmes, educational programmes, as well as MA and doctoral pathways. His doctoral thesis explored the deployment of teaching assistants by trainee teachers. Robert is a member of National Association of Primary Education (NAPE) and is the association's journal editor.

Miller, D. A., Kosek, A., & Morgan, R. (2025). 'A university should be a place open to the exchange of ideas, not one of censorship': Balancing equity, diversity, and inclusion and free speech in academia, *Equity in Education & Society*, 0(0). Available at: https://doi.org/10.1177/27526461251371312

Gibson, P., Morgan, R., & Brett, A. (2024). *Primary teacher solutions*. Abingdon: Routledge.

Morgan, R. (2022). 'Myth busting in the contemporary primary classroom', in Ogier, S. (ed), *A Broad & Balanced Curriculum in Primary Schools*. 2nd edn. London: SAGE, pp. 296–307.

Morgan, R. (2021). 'Religious Education; a freedom to teach creatively', in McDonald, R. and Gibson, P. (eds), *Inspiring Primary Learners: Insights and Inspiration Across the Curriculum*. London: Routledge, pp. 186–201.

Morgan, R. (2019). 'The practice of the deployment of teaching assistants by trainee teachers during classroom teaching experiences: an issue of negotiation', *Primary First*, (26), pp. 18–25.

1

INTRODUCTION

═══════════════ Chapter Aims ═══════════════

- What is this book trying to achieve?
- Why is this book structured as it is?
- Who is this book for, and who is it written by?
- Why do trainee teachers need do a research project?

WHAT IS THIS BOOK TRYING TO ACHIEVE?

This book is intended to alleviate, or at least minimise, any fear or apprehension that you as an education student may have about undertaking a research project, whether your concern is regarding vocabulary, methodologies, the literature review, ethics, data collection, or data analysis, or perhaps you just lack the experience to be confident about the whole thing. The reason many students are apprehensive about the research project is because a dissertation, of which your research project is an example, usually comes at the end of a period of study, and so it is easy to see this as a pinnacle of academic achievement, and potentially one that 'has to be got right' if you are to secure a satisfying degree classification. But the word 'right' is unhelpful in this context. Three students could each successfully approach the same research question in very different ways, and all three of them could be 'right'. This is because there is no 'right' in research. There is only 'appropriate'. This book will help you to recognise important principles about school-based research, and therefore to make helpful decisions about what constitutes appropriateness in all aspects of your research project.

The majority of this book is common sense, based on years of experience on the part of the authors. It seeks to help you see the undertaking of a research project as an opportunity and a privilege, not as a hoop to jump through. After all, were it not a compulsory part of your course, it is unlikely that you would unilaterally choose to undertake an original piece of research, with its demands of ethics and transparent processes. It would be so much easier and safer for you to stay within your existing experiences, particularly if you have been achieving satisfying grades for your course submissions up to now. But that is the point. A research project forces you into new cognitive and organisational areas, and this book will give you a road map. Strong research is logical and can be planned step-by-step, and while it is very likely that there will be surprises along the way, this book will help you tell the difference between unwelcome surprises which need a direct response, and welcome ones, which are to be celebrated. This book will help you to know how to deal with both.

WHY IS THIS BOOK STRUCTURED AS IT IS?

You will be able to see how this book is structured and what specific things it covers from the index, and you may be surprised at the order of some of the chapters, For example, consideration of your research project's introduction and abstract is not included until Chapter 11, but there is a reason for that. Since even you will not know until the end of your project exactly what happened during it, it makes sense for the introduction to be one of the last things you write. This book is not intended to be rigidly chronological in terms of the order that you do things in, but broadly speaking, the early chapters cover things that should inform your initial thinking and planning, and will therefore direct the later more hands-on parts of your project. There is no hard and fast rule about whether you should write your literature review before or after your methodology, but we would strongly advise you to achieve clarity about the focus you are looking to explore, what you are trying to achieve within that focus, what research question you are trying to answer, and the nature of the data you are intending to collect before writing either. This is why Chapters 2 and 3 will be fundamental to your early thinking, and why the chapter on ethics (Chapter 4) comes before the chapters about either methodology or the literature review. One of the most common features of early tutorials regarding a research project is supervisors stopping students from running headlong into a methodology before they have even decided what it is they are trying to achieve or discover, and why. It is also instructive to realise that just in terms of size, the ethics chapter is one of the biggest in the book. This is because it is not possible to get a really high grade (90%+) without strong ethics. Do not skimp there.

The ethics chapter includes information about what things you must consider when designing a research project but also contains examples of the experiences of students whose research project grades were substantially enhanced or seriously weakened by their respective strong or thoughtless approaches to ethical aspects of research design. The fact that you need to secure ethical approval is not the big thing regarding the ethics of your study. Do not think for a moment that securing ethical approval is the target, and that approval is where your interest in ethics starts and finishes. Ethics will impact every aspect of your research project, not least because if you are empathetic and think through the experiences that you will be giving your participants you will be able to recruit and retain people who will be happy to share rich data with you because you treat them well, you ask them to do things they are comfortable with and enjoy doing, and there are no unexpected surprises. By contrast, if you see them primarily as a source of data and ask them to do things which are inaccessible, unenjoyable, unexpected, or which unthinkingly damage their self-esteem your data will be at best thin and at worst non-existent. Ethics need not be a minefield if you carefully think through the implications of your study for the experiences of your participants and the settings your research is undertaken in.

WHO IS THIS BOOK FOR, AND WHO IS IT WRITTEN BY?

This book is written by two university senior lecturers who between them have over thirty years' experience of leading research project modules at undergraduate and postgraduate levels. Both authors hold doctorates in the field of education research and have a history of research publication (some of their selected publications are at the end of the previous chapter). They have taught extensively on research project modules, and between them have supervised hundreds of education students, usually either trainee teachers whose courses led towards Qualified Teacher Status, or experienced education professionals seeking MAs or doctorates. As a result, the authors of this book know the most common or tricky questions students ask about research projects throughout the process from beginning to end. They know what support or advice to give. They know how to stretch the more able students and to support those who are struggling. They know what works in a school-based research project, and what does not. They have also seen the most common mistakes research students make (usually ethical and/or methodological) and have gained the experience to put support and information in place to pre-empt these mistakes from happening (at least for those students who choose to listen and to be advised). This book is a crystallisation of their experience. Since you are already reading this book, you are almost certainly to be numbered amongst those students who will listen and take advice. As a result, your research project and its consequent grade will be improved a lot by the reading of this book.

This book is primarily written for students on teacher training courses or perhaps on MA courses, and who are required to undertake a school-based research project, usually in the later stages of their course. It is a book which will inform all the many choices you will need to make from initial thoughts to submission.

In every chapter, this book deliberately gives lots of examples and asks you to consider reflective questions along the way, to shape your thinking or to apply context to your own research ideas. You will read the stories of students who have met with triumph and disaster, and we explore why. For example, within some of these stories we identify ways in which seemingly innocuous methodological features resulted in enhanced grades or served to significantly weaken the project. In reading this book you will be able to learn from the sort of mistakes or successes experienced by those who have gone before you. All the examples that we give relate to the experiences of students who were ultimately successful, albeit with various degrees of success. Having said that, some of the students' experiences we share with you have been conflated or the settings changed. Some scenarios are amplified, adapted or repurposed, but each is indicative of real and common errors or successes that real students have experienced. All the scenarios we present happened to (or by) one or more real people in one form or another, but no real person or actual research project is represented, depicted or quoted. All names have been invented.

The book is written in plain English and is designed to be practical and very easy to read. It is not a typical book about research. To this end it is not peppered with references, citations and theoretical positions. There is nothing here that is so hard to understand you will need to unpick it with other students or with a tutor. Yes, this book does explore difficult sounding words like 'ontology' and 'epistemology' (Chapter 2), but only because these things are important if you want a good grade in your research project, and the book does this in a way that demystifies these words. There is nothing complicated about ontology or epistemology, other than the fact that these are words which we as a society rarely use, so you may initially lack the context to know about them. This book is big on context. We as authors do not dumb down, but equally we do not overly complicate either.

WHY DO TRAINEE TEACHERS NEED DO A RESEARCH PROJECT?

Many trainee teachers are surprised when they learn that a large (often 30 credits) assessed research project module is a significant component of their course. Since it is a module that attracts so many academic credits, students often ask themselves and each other 'What has this to do with my teaching? How will this help my pedagogy, my subject knowledge, or my classroom management? How will this make me a better teacher? Why is the demand for an understanding of research ethics an appropriate focus on an Initial Teacher Training course'?

The answer to these questions is threefold. First, a dissertation is an established component of nearly all degree courses in most disciplines. Degrees are no longer exclusively about the acquisition of subject-specific skills and knowledge within an identified discipline, restrained and bounded by high windowless walls and rigid parameters. Modern degrees are designed to broaden the mind, expand horizons, develop transferable skills for a flexible labour market, and to foster a community of researchers so that students leave with a facility for enquiry and curiosity. Very few students hold such a low expectation of an education degree that they seek merely to be passively fed with knowledge; to be told by a more experienced other what effective practice is and what it is not; to be mentored to perform established mechanics of being a classroom practitioner; or to be told specifically how to deliver the current priorities in government education policy. Instead, most students seek some autonomy, to explore their own interests, and to develop advanced academic and cognitive skills. That is why the dissertation is an established component in a degree. Enough of answering pre-determined essay titles. Enough of being told what to read. It's time to shine. It's time to think for yourself.

Second, schools and classrooms are organic places. You have probably already discovered that things that work for you in the classroom one day may not work the next; or things that worked in one setting or age group seem less effective in another. In your response to these situations, you have two options, each very different from the other, and only one of which you can be proud. The first is you can unthinkingly shrug your shoulders and carry on regardless, unconcerned and passively accepting that things happen as they happen and hoping that they might improve or become more consistent next time. The alternative is to be active, to try to ascertain why things happen or happened, to have a curiosity about what works and why, to introduce and monitor changes to your classroom or your management processes to improve the experiences of your learners and to be confident in your professional choices. You will be able to be confident in doing this because your research project will have taught you the basics of research. You will experiment with your classroom practice in a systematic and ethically informed way so that no one, especially no child, will get inadvertently hurt, physically, or emotionally, even in a small way. In an assessed research project, you are being given the opportunity to take that second option, to develop the skills and understandings you will need to research and make informed changes in your professional practice successfully, and what's more you will be earning credits towards your degree or teaching qualification while you do it. What a gift. Suddenly, your research project looks to be an essential component of your teacher training, rather than being the odd one out in a series of otherwise relevant teacher training modules.

Third, the research project enables the really strong students, the thinkers, the problem solvers and the innovators to be identified from the merely talented, the comfortably competent, the unimaginative, or the academically idle. Your research project can transform you from being a passive consumer of knowledge to an active producer. A highly successful project will evidence critical thinking which assesses, questions and evaluates assumptions, makes evidence-based conclusions, and considers different perspectives (perhaps the views of your participants will differ markedly from each other, or from your own preconceptions). Your research project is an opportunity for you to demonstrate skills at evaluation, and to apply knowledge to a specific situation.

When all students are answering the same essay title (and that title is necessarily safe and risk-minimised because it is designed to enable all students to be successful) it is hard for individuals to evidence originality or imagination. All the talk in the playground is about that one essay title, and the less able students benefit from hearing the insight of the more able. That is not a bad thing in itself. If you consciously practice the use of mixed-ability groups in your classroom you are deliberately engineering a situation which results in the more able children leading the conversations while the less able benefit from their leadership. We call it social constructivism, and it is to be encouraged. But in a higher education environment it does mask the truly able student, the independent learner, the high-flyer, the student capable of a grade in excess of 90%. So, to encourage this, when you as a student can and must choose your own focus and identify your own parameters within a field (and that in itself is a difficult academic skill); and when you are obliged to choose and implement a methodology, then the really big marks are available to you, and that is what university tutors like to award if they can. In situations where you are given a set essay question, much of the hard work has already been done for you by your tutor, and you cannot display your understanding of a field by your formulation of an insightful research question or the identification of an interesting or original research area. If you have no curiosity about a particular aspect of education, or no preference about what your research project might focus upon, of course you will find the pre-prepared essay title to be attractive. You will not have had to think for yourself. Now, and instead, in your research project you are forced to do just that. If you can do it, and do it well, you will be handsomely rewarded by a good grade. Many students love that situation and thrive on it. Others (still the majority) are a bit anxious about it at first but go on to cope perfectly well and ulti-mately enjoy it. Some do not know where to start and need a bit of help to get going and regular support along the way. A very few panic and may even complain that they did not expect to have to pay all this money to go to university, only to then have to do everything for themselves.

So that is why a research project is an appropriate and necessary component of a teacher training course. The teaching profession does not need a new generation of compliant automatons. It needs independent thinkers, enthusiasts, motivators, self-assured organisers, problem solvers, and innovators. This is as true within a single classroom (micro-level) as it is within national policy (macro-level). To be an innovator you first need an understanding of what change is desirable, and the ability to collect and analyse data to give you the evidence to support and monitor that change. Your research project will foster the skills you need to be impactful within your chosen profession. We wish you well with it, but of course in reality, you do not need our good wishes. You need good advice with helpful examples, and that is what this book will give you.

By the way, there is no such thing as a 'born researcher'. There are no mysterious and specific research skills which you must learn quickly if you are to be successful, and which are only applicable and useful in a research context. Yes, it helps to be very well-organised, to be properly resourced, to have a plan and to stick to it where possible or desirable, to be methodical, to have good time management skills, and to have a good reason for doing things, but the same is true of baking a cake. It is good to make sure no one gets hurt as you pursue your interests, but that is also true when driving. It is good to be able to list, sort and separate different pieces of information, and to apply that analysis to a given setting or situation, but that also applies to a visit to a supermarket or to booking a holiday. You are already practising research skills every day. This book will help you to recognise the ways in which the useful life skills that you already have can be applied to a very specific research outcome. It will explain research words you may not have come across before and tell you how they apply to your already well-developed armoury of relevant skills and experience, and to your own very individual perception of knowledge and reality.

Research is never easy, but it need not be ridiculously difficult either, if you know firstly what the most common errors are and how to avoid them; and secondly what routes and methods are likely to be the most promising for success. This book will provide you with both.

2

THE NATURE OF KNOWLEDGE: WHAT IS IT ·TO KNOW OR LEARN SOMETHING?

━━━━━━━━━━ **Chapter Aims** ━━━━━━━━━━

This chapter will explore:

- The nature of knowledge.
- Definitions and applications of the words ontology and epistemology.
- An example of how ontology and epistemology will impact your research project (whether you are aware of it or not).
- To what extent is social science scientific?

━━━━━━━━━━ **Reflective Questions 2.1** ━━━━━━━━━━

- How certain can you be of what you know?
- Is there a difference between knowledge and truth?
- How would your background influence what you know?
- How would knowledge within a community or school shape its culture and values?
- Can the desire to know something ever be unethical?

INTRODUCTION

Knowledge is not value-free. Everything you know has been learnt, inherited, or filtered through multiple lenses, including your gender, ethnicity, age, nationality, upbringing, race, class, health, and opportunity. Knowledge is rarely an independent thing. It must have context, and there must be someone to know or have known it.

Your course tutor is likely to have used the words ontology and epistemology with you. These are words you may have heard before, but they may not have consciously and directly affected your life until now, even if you are training as a teacher. This chapter will explain these two terms, and, more importantly, explain why they are essential to your research project. These words will impact your study whether you are aware of them or not, but your grade is likely to be enhanced if you can demonstrate your awareness of them beyond merely explaining what the words mean. Defining them is easy. If you want to get the high grades, you will need to show how they have impacted your methodology. Do not worry. That is not hard either, and we will explain how and why.

ONTOLOGY

Ontology explores what can be known. It is a consideration of the nature of knowledge. The word 'knowledge' is an unhelpful umbrella term for any number of things that inform the way we live and the choices we each make. Here are some examples of things I know.

1 The Titanic sank in 1912.
2 Water boils at 100°C.
3 The best route from Southeast London to Sheffield.
4 My wife loves me.
5 How to ride a bike.
6 Not to touch a frayed electrical wire.
7 How to dress appropriately.

I 'know' each of these things, but are they all 'knowledge'? Well yes, they are, but of very different types.

The first statement is a fact. There are records. It cannot be disputed. It will always be so.

The second looks like a fact but is not. Water does indeed boil at 100°C, but only at sea level. The higher the altitude, the lower the boiling point. So, this is a fact, but only if you are by the sea. If a fact is location dependent, there are more exceptions than rules, which is not helpful in a fact.

The third is an opinion. There are any number of routes and modes of transport to get me from Southeast London to Sheffield, and if I choose to go by train, car, helicopter, motorbike, or to walk, that is up to me, as is the route I end up taking. The statement is knowledge, in that I know what my choice of transport and route are most likely to be, but it is possible that I could be persuaded by you should you choose to advise me otherwise. The knowledge is peculiar to my preference, experience, budget, opportunity, and timescale. You are likely to hold different views to me on the subject, but if that is the case, even if I consider you to be wrong, we can still be friends.

The fourth is a perception. It is reinforced to me on an (almost) daily basis in the way my wife and I live, but if I asked her for empirical proof that she loves me, I would get a withering look. This knowledge is a (happily) strongly held perception, but it is there-fore subjective. Nonetheless, its subjectivity does not diminish its validity or impor-tance, and it is certainly more important to me than my empirical knowledge of the year the Titanic sank. So, can knowledge be subjective? Yes. Absolutely. This is one reason why you need not fear subjectivity in your research project.

The fifth is a skill. I learnt it by doing, and by falling off my bike until I got it right.

The sixth is advisory and consequential. I am free to touch the frayed wire or not. The world is full of advisories for which there may be consequences (laws, sell-by-dates, stand on the right). This knowledge is only knowledge once I understand why I should not touch the wire. Being compliant to the advice not to touch is not in itself knowledge about electrical wires. This statement is only knowledge once I understand the conse-quence of the advice.

The seventh and last is to do with culture and identity, and this is the most value-laden of the seven statements. I 'know' how to dress as a white, middle-aged, western-European man. Again, it is knowledge which is individual to me. And even here, I dress differently for different occasions. My 'knowledge' is very societally com-plex. It is about me knowing how to feel comfortable, or powerful, or wanting to dress down to fit in, or to dress up to respect the people I am with. I know how to do that in the society in which I live (and only in that society). The anticipated majority demo-graphic of readers of this book is such that you are probably not a middle-aged man. You are probably a good deal younger than me, or you are female, or both. As such, you also know how to dress in the society in which we both live, but you would prefer not to dress as I dress. Importantly, you would not try to correct or criticise my dress, nor I yours. You would probably not offer an alternative opinion as you might when critiquing my choice of the best route to Sheffield. But if you did offer a critical or formative opinion about the way I dress, or I on yours, it is unlikely we would remain friends. The knowledge of how one might dress is knowledge that has been culturally learnt (nurtured? imposed?) and it is very sensitive and context dependent. Strong views are held, and all of them different. But, if they are all different, can this be knowledge? Again, yes. Knowledge is not truth.

So here we have seven different types of knowledge. It is not an exhaustive list, and there are other types of knowledge (for example, intrapersonal knowledge of one's own feelings and well-being; or conduct on a sports field), but you can immediately see how an awareness of ontology, of what can be known, might have an impact on your research project, and as a direct result, your research question. Are you trying to identify facts, or perhaps you are looking for opinions, or perceptions, behaviours, skills, or attitudes? Are you trying to explore an area of knowledge that might involve deep ontological sensitivities, in which case ethical considerations must be hugely height-ened? Once you have decided upon a field or a question to explore, it would be a good idea to consider in your research project's methodology what sorts of 'knowledge' or data such a question might generate, and as a corollary, how you might go about col-lecting that data. For example, you may be of the view that to get a good grade, subjectivity should be avoided at all costs in your research project. That is a common (and incorrect) thought amongst new researchers, but classrooms are organic places, full of people with diverse ages, skills, preferences, and experiences. Can the question you want to ask or the area you want to explore be looked at most effectively by the objective measuring or counting of things? In our experience the most interesting questions to be asked about a school or classroom do not require facts, measurement or counting. What is the nature of what you want to know? What are you trying to find out? These are ontological questions.

Imagine how impressed your marker will be when you go beyond a simple identification that 'ontology is about the nature of knowledge' and go on to explain how your awareness of different types of knowledge has influenced the design of your project. You can see that your research project grade is going up already, and we are only in Chapter 2 of this book.

EPISTEMOLOGY

Epistemology explores how we know things. Whereas ontology considers the nature of knowledge, epistemology considers the filters and processes through which those things can be known. For example, the way I learnt how to read was very different from the way I learnt to ride a bike. I have never forgotten either. By contrast there are things I learnt at school (the names of cloud types, for example, and their relationship to this afternoon's weather) that were learnt by rote, and are now neither remembered, nor impactful on my life. Epistemology is about acquisition and application of that umbrella term we call knowledge.

Wittgenstein effectively articulated the difference between ontology and epistemology (although he was discussing the nature of language, not research methodology). He differentiated between problems of ignorance and problems of confusion (Hart, 2018: 229), and in your research project, you should do this too. Are you exploring a research question because you want to know more about it (a problem of ignorance)? In this case you are taking an ontological approach, seeking to gather facts, or information, and for an identified purpose relating to knowledge (yours, or a group of people's). Or are you exploring a research question because you want to achieve greater understanding of it (a problem of confusion)? Here you are taking an epistemological approach. The facts are known, and you are seeking clarification, contextualisation, or insight (for you, or for a group).

Each of the seven types of knowledge listed above come under the banner of knowledge (ontology), but none of those things can be known in the same way (epistemology). Note that epistemology is not the same thing as pedagogy. Pedagogy is the science of learning and teaching. Epistemology is about knowing. There are subtle differences. Effective teachers are likely to have a keen awareness of pedagogy, which will consciously impact such things as classroom layout and organisation, and lesson planning and assessment. Pedagogy tends to relate to individuals or classes, and to individual or series of learning events or learning intentions. It is short-term and immediate. By contrast, as well as knowledge and skills, epistemology can embrace things such as values, behaviours, and attitudes. It tests new knowledge against what is already known.

Whilst ontology explores what can be known, epistemology explores how we know things, and this will impact on your research project, if you let it. If you are interviewing people, an awareness of the difference between ontology and epistemology can inform the phrasing of your questions, or the sequence in which you ask them. An example would be illuminating here.

DIFFERENCES BETWEEN A PREDOMINANTLY ONTOLOGICAL APPROACH TO A RESEARCH PROJECT, AND A PREDOMINANTLY EPISTEMOLOGICAL ONE

Molly and Owain are trainee teachers in different schools, and for their research projects, each is interested in finding teachers' views on important factors in the learning and teaching of early reading, by which they both mean phonics. They each have decided to interview Year 1 and Reception teachers, and they have planned to ask the following contrasting series of questions. Consider the differences in responses (data) the participating teachers might give to each (see Table 2.1).

Table 2.1 Ontological and Epistemological Approaches

Molly	Owain
• What do you think are the most important aspects of teaching phonics to Year 1 [or Reception] children?	• What do you think are the most important aspects of teaching reading to Year 1 [or Reception] children?
• What resources do you find most or least useful?	• What makes you say that? Can you tell me more?
• How do you go about adapting your teaching for children who fall behind in phonics, or struggle to understand?	• What makes a good reader at this young age?
• Is handwriting important at Year 1 [Reception]?	• What is your number one priority when teaching reading at Year 1 [or Reception]?
• What makes phonics the best way to teach reading?	• Why is that?
• What do children find hardest in learning phonics?	• What place does phonics have in the overall teaching of reading?
• What do you find hardest to teach in phonics?	• What advice would you give to a newly qualified teacher about children's learning of early reading?
	• Do you enjoy teaching reading? Tell me why.

Molly and Owain have very different ontological and epistemological approaches here. Molly is trying to reduce the variables. She knows what she wants to find out, and she knows how she is going to do it. Molly wants a research project where she can analyse the responses comparatively, perhaps even using tables to catalogue how the teachers respond to her last two questions, (two questions that she is very pleased with). She plans to structure her data analysis by presenting responses to each question in turn, which she will be able to do because she has left her participants very little wriggle room. She secretly hopes that the teachers might disclose attitudes and priorities which she herself holds or she can strongly relate to, thus confirming that she has made good progress in her teacher training course, and she will go on to make a good teacher of phonics. She has an interview for a teaching post coming up, and she hopes to use the teachers' responses to inform any question she is asked about phonics, which she thinks is bound to come up. Molly knows she has planned a strong research project because she is helpfully leading her participants by the hand, asking very specific questions around very specific things, which constantly focus their responses onto her chosen research question. Molly has purposely arranged a very tidy research project so her supervisor and marker will be impressed. She is confident that a good grade is pretty much guaranteed.

Molly is being very ontological, and very safe. She knows what she knows, and she is not all that interested in exploring how she might audit that knowledge by allowing new thoughts to test them. As a result of her own experiences in school placements, even before asking a question to her participants she has already decided what views about which areas are most likely to be held by teachers regarding important factors in the learning and teaching of early reading (phonics, resources, adaptive teaching, and links between reading and writing), and so she has arranged for the teachers to articulate their thoughts around these pre-selected areas. She has already written her literature review and structured it around these four areas which she searched for specifically, using them as keywords in the university's library search databases, so she is eagerly anticipating that her literature and her data will happily resonate. Given the way she has a strangle hold on the direction of travel throughout the interviews, she is probably right.

Molly is daring to dream that a first-class degree might be a possibility. About this, she is probably wrong, also because of her intentional stranglehold on proceedings. Disappointment may be just around the corner. Her title speaks of teachers' views on important factors in the learning and teaching of early reading. Molly's methodology is using her participants to reinforce her own view.

Owain has not done any of that. Owain is not sure what he is going to find out from the teachers, but he hopes it will be interesting and will inform his future professional practice. He has chosen to ask questions that the participants can take in any direction, and so he is a bit scared that there won't be any coherence or obvious patterns within the data. What he does know is that his findings are likely to faithfully disclose the attitudes and priorities of his participants, whatever those attitudes might be. He is secretly hoping to find attitudes and priorities that he had not previous thought of himself, or responses that might help to clarify aspects about the teaching of early reading that he is conflicted about. Perhaps one of the teachers will hold maverick or unfashionable views which will make his data analysis interesting. He does not yet know how he will organise his data analysis chapter, but he will decide that once he has collected all the responses. He is starting to regret taking such an unstructured approach as he fears his supervisor will not be at all impressed at the lack of guidance afforded to his participants. He needs a good grade if he is going to secure the upper second-class degree he and his family have been hoping for, but he is not at all confident. He wishes now that his study was more like his friend Molly's. In his darkest moments, Owain even fears failure. If that happened, what is he to say to his family, and to the school where he has been offered a teaching position in September?

Owain's approach, in contrast to Molly's, is very epistemological. He feels he is taking risks, perhaps recklessly (he is not). Owain is not entirely sure that he knows what he knows about priorities in early reading but wants to see where his rather unformed attitudes might sit within the views of several other teaching professionals who he respects and whose experience he wants to interrogate. He seeks understanding and insight. He wants to see where his rather conflicted views on the preeminent place of phonics in the teaching of reading sit with those of more experienced professionals. He has been reading around the subject of early reading but is a bit baffled by the variety of well-argued attitudes and policies he has found there, and he wants to apply his reading to real-life situations. Ironically, although he wishes that his study was more like Molly's, they are both likely to be a bit surprised when Owain's overall grade is at least as good, if not rather higher, than Molly's.

Their attitudes to ontology and epistemology (conscious or otherwise) have led them to very different research interview designs. This is why, if students of research projects want the top grades, they need to demonstrate an understanding not only of what the terms ontology and epistemology mean, but to acknowledge why and how these terms have informed and impacted their studies. If Owain was more conscious of epistemology, he would have been less concerned about his choice of interview questions. Indeed, he would have openly celebrated the reasons he chose them, and in his submission would have made a virtue of them, and of his broad reading around the subject which led to his conflicted responses to school priorities in the field of early reading. He would also have had fewer sleepless nights worrying about failure. Had Molly been more conscious of her adherence to ontology, she might have allowed her participants a much freer rein in the interviews, and she would also have read much more widely rather than simply undertaking a blinkered search for sources to validate her own preconceptions.

TO WHAT EXTENT IS SOCIAL SCIENCE SCIENTIFIC?

The phrase 'research project' can itself lead students in unhelpful directions, because many come to their project thinking of research in overtly scientific terms. They think they must prove or confirm something in a way that if someone else replicated the study, the same outcome or findings would be realised. Research in schools, however, falls predominantly under the umbrella of social sciences because schools are social places, so the question arises, to what extent can social sciences claim to be Science?

Like so many things in universities, the answer to this question depends upon a definition of the word 'science'.

We noted above that if you have a strong belief that knowledge is limited to what can be described as objective reality then your research project will be full of numbers, charts and graphs. But in our view, for your research project to be scientific, it is not necessary to seek to discover facts, or to count and measure things. It is true that, by definition, social sciences explore human behaviours, preferences and perceptions, and therefore social scientists are working in fields that abound with variables and inconsistencies, but they do this using systematic and evidence-based approaches, and it is this that makes social sciences scientific.

There are two approaches to the 'Is social science really Science?' question. The first approach denies it, reserving science to be the identification of the incontestable, with a consequent isolation of variables and the pursuit of replicable outcomes. The second accepts it, seeing the term 'science' as a tool kit, rather than an end in itself. Social scientists, of whom you are now one, seek to undertake their research scientifically, in that they apply rigorous research ethics; they underpin their research right from the beginning by demonstrating their understanding of the literature surrounding the research question; they use tried and tested methods and tools of neutral data collection; and they seek ways to analyse data impartially. They conduct their research systematically.

So yes, social science can claim to be scientific because those of us who are engaged in it behave scientifically. It is our use of methods and checks that make it so. Indeed, we would argue that for this reason some aspects of social sciences are even more scientifically demanding than those found in the natural sciences. For example, compare the ethics of doing research with children or adults who have learning or physical difficulties with the ethics of researching how to maximise the battery range of an electric car. It is true that both contain ethical aspects, but an ethics committee is not going to disallow the latter because of its recruitment procedures or its potentially invasive practices which may negatively impact a battery's rights or sensitivities. Social sciences must uphold scientific procedures to a very high standard if they are to be authentic and valid.

By the way, if you find yourself in conversation with someone who is a staunch adherent of knowledge as objective reality, as the authors of this book sometimes have the misfortune to do with our colleagues from other faculties, do not even try to convince them. Moral high ground is rarely more obviously claimed and more rigorously adhered to than by researchers in the natural or mathematical sciences when they discuss the nature and status of social sciences. They have no intention of yielding even an accurately measured inch. Claiming to be in jest when they speak about the methodological superiority of their objective paradigm, they tend to sneer and make disparaging remarks about our allowance for (and celebration of) subjectivity in research, however you must not be cowed or discouraged. It is best to simply change the subject or walk away. It is a mystery to the writers of this book how these colleagues identify through the exclusive pursuit of objective reality, and without any consideration of human perceptions, the effects that their teaching and assessment practices have on their students (or how they explore the extent to which their students would agree).

We would argue instead that if we as a research community restrict ourselves to applying a definition of 'science' only to a study of those things that can be measured, weighed or counted (as for example a physicist might), then we deny ourselves the possibility of exploring in a systematic way things of truly human interest. There would be no theories of learning development, and no subsequent impact on pedagogy, school design, or resource use. There would be no theoretical frameworks, such as Bronfenbrenner's ecological systems theory, Kolb's experiential learning theory, or Bruner's Theory of Cognitive Development. There would be no recognised methods for the analysis of qualitative data such as Braun and Clarke's thematic analysis. If educationalists had succumbed, intimidated by the dismissive accusations of statistical unreliability from our friends on the objective reality side of the research spectrum, there would be no theories of constructivism, social constructivism or behaviourism, and all because no one had the confidence to apply scientific principles to the study of human behaviour or development. In our view, educationalists have a duty to undertake social science, and to systematically question and analyse what we do in schools, early years settings and colleges to improve the experience and effectiveness of our practices in an evidence-based way. It is a noble pursuit, and it is a science because we do it scientifically.

◼◼◼◼◼◼ Activity 2.1 ◼◼◼◼◼◼

1 We suggest that you keep notes to reflect on your learning throughout your research project. For example, how do you learn or know things in your likely research area? What are your ontological and epistemological stances regarding your possible research area? A good component to the conclusion to your research project would be not only an identification of what you have learnt about the research field, but also what you have learnt about research methods and vocabulary. It is easy to forget milestones or moments of success or clarity, so keep a simple diary reflecting on your progress.
2 Discuss epistemological questions with fellow students such as 'what is knowledge', or 'what are the most important things I know, and how do I know them?' or 'how important is the sort of knowledge that can be contained in a curriculum'.

SUMMARY

The big messages we hope you take from this chapter are:

- The word 'knowledge' is an unhelpful umbrella term for the variety of things we all 'know'.
- Knowledge is very often subjective, and that is OK. Knowledge is not certain. Knowledge is not truth.

- If you accept that a great deal of knowledge is subjective, you need have no fear of elements of subjectivity in your research project. There is no need to prove things in your submission. In social science research, perceptions are not the poor relations of facts.
- The most interesting things to research in school are rarely measurable.
- You should be aware of the difference between problems of ignorance and problems of confusion.

FURTHER READING

Crotty, M. (1998). *The foundations of social research*. London: SAGE. Introduction.
This book links methodology and theory with great clarity and precision, showing students and researchers how to navigate the maze of conflicting terminology.

Grey, D. (2021). *Doing research in the real world*. 5th edn. London: SAGE – Chapter 2.
This book helps you build your knowledge of theory and methods and offers straightforward guidance to empower you to make good research decisions and learn best practice in a step-by-step basis.

Hart, C. (2018). *Doing a literature review*. 2nd edn. London: SAGE Chapter 7.
In this chapter, Hart explores and celebrates (amongst other things) the way a research question can be usefully couched as a problem of ignorance or a problem of confusion. This distinction can inform and strengthen your methodology.

Thomas, G. (2023). *How to do your research project*. 4th edn. London: SAGE – Chapter 5.
This book is reader friendly and explains matters easily, but is not specific to research in schools.

Wilson, E. (ed.) (2017). *School-based research*. 3rd edn. London: SAGE.
This is a thorough and thoughtful guide to the research process, covering qualitative, quantitative, and mixed research methods. It guides you through research design, data collection and analysis and how to write up your research findings.

3

TYPES OF RESEARCH IN SCHOOLS

━━━━━━━━━━ **Chapter Aims** ━━━━━━━━━━

This chapter will explore:

- Common research vocabulary.
- What is a research paradigm, and do I need one?
- What is a case study, and action research?
- Intrinsic and instrumental case studies, with examples.
- How paradigms and research design are connected, with examplers.
- Research with human participants, with suggestions.
- Research without human participants, with examples.

INTRODUCTION

The vocabulary surrounding research can be very daunting to new researchers. Your course tutor may have used the phrase 'research paradigm' which has possibly made you anxious before you even start. You may not know what a case study is, and whether your research project is an example of one. You wonder whether 'qualitative' is a research method (it is not).

This chapter explores the vocabulary surrounding the most common types of research undertaken by students on the research project modules we have led, and it also responds to the most common questions students have asked us over the years. We also explore research with and without human participants.

WHAT IS A PARADIGM?

You will, knowingly or unknowingly, adopt a research paradigm in your work. A paradigm is an ideological or philosophical framework within which a researcher chooses to operate, and the paradigm(s) you choose will reflect your priorities and attitudes regarding the nature of knowledge (Chapter 2). For example, if your view of research is that things need to be proved, and empirically demonstrated or tested, then your research design will reflect that, and you will go on to count, measure, and tally things that can be counted, measured and tallied. You will favour an empirical, quantitative paradigm. Conversely, if your view of research is that knowledge is rarely a constant and must be experienced through a lens of human experience, then your design will reflect that, and you will observe, interview and investigate things that can be observed, discussed and investigated. As such, you will go on to adopt an interpretative, qualitative paradigm. There are no right or wrong paradigms. There are simply appropriate and inappropriate ones, depending on your research focus or setting. Your chosen paradigm will inform the methods within each (Chapter 5).

Overwhelmingly, where trainee teachers have involved human participants in the many projects we have supervised, the most common paradigm is interpretivist, and the most prominent feature of this is the collection qualitative (non-numeric) data. An interpretivist approach does not seek to prove or disprove anything but simply observes and reports a given phenomenon or situation in one or more settings. Common data collection tools are questionnaires, interviews, focus groups, and observation. Sometimes participants may be asked to keep diaries. The data identifies and reveals subjective things such as attitudes, perceptions, preferences, tensions, and behaviours.

Less commonly, students will choose to use or include a positivist paradigm, the most prominent feature being the collection of quantitative (numeric) data. Common data collection tools are experiments, polls, surveys, and tallies. Research project students are often attracted by this approach initially because they unnecessarily fear that bias and subjectivity in research are bad things, and so they consider that subjectivity will be minimised by objective measurements. There is only partial truth in this because the thing that you choose to measure (for example, how many children make use of a particular mathematical resource; the frequency of use; for how long; and for what purpose) is decided by you, based on your own subjective interests, intentions and purposes. But also, more significantly, your commitment to measuring things may prevent you from exploring a much more interesting question (such as whether the children found the mathematical resource helpful, or motivating, or easy to use, or even whether they knew what the resource was for. Is it possible that they spent so much time with it because they were completely baffled by it? Your counting, timing, and measuring will not identify any of that).

You should not feel, therefore, that the use of a positivist paradigm strengthens your project by default. It may well be useful to count or measure things, but do not feel obliged to include such an approach unless your research question makes it at least attractive, and preferably compelling.

Examples of Research Project Titles Which Could Allow a Quantitative Component to Be Useful

- Reading preferences held by Key Stage 2 girls with similar reading age scores.
- How can stamina for a class of Year 8 children be increased in PE lessons?
- Which children are selected for assembly prizes, and why?

- The frequency and length of playground equipment use analysed by age and gender.
- Can a school's travel to school policy have an effect on reducing car usage?
- How to increase parental engagement and attendance in mathematics workshops.

━━━━━━━ Reflective Questions 3.1 ━━━━━━━

- Which paradigm would you consider influences your intended research question, if you already have one, and why? How would the chosen paradigm be suitable for your data collection methods and participants?

RESEARCH DESIGN: CASE STUDIES AND ACTION RESEARCH

Having identified which paradigm best suits an exploration of your chosen field, or whether you are going to use aspects of both, you will next want to identify a method. Do not worry that you have not yet established a specific research question. That will come later (Chapter 5). Statistically, from the many research projects we have supervised, it is most likely that for your research project you will choose to undertake a case study, so to get the good grades you will need to demonstrate to your marker your understanding of what that means.

The fundamental difference between a case study and action research is that case studies have a focus which is predominantly concentrated on a single group or phenomenon, looked at within a single and distinct window of time. In a case study you are not seeking to compare pre-intervention and post-intervention change, or to undertake an experiment. You are not trying to solve or mitigate a perceived problem. You are merely identifying things as they are. You might discover participants' views or behaviours, but you are not seeking to change them. Case studies tend to be short-term, which is why they are an attractive design for research project students.

But what is a case? As far as your research project is concerned, a case can be anything that forms an identifiable unit, with clear parameters. For example, in a research project the case could be a class or year group; or children in a lunchtime chess club; or teachers who run lunchtime clubs; Learning Support Assistants; a subject department; a school; an education authority. A case can also be bounded by a period, for example, a study of a class over a week or half-term. For example, you might seek to shadow a Year 9 class for a day or two, and note the variety of their learning experiences, or energy levels, or behaviours. But a case does not have to be made up by people. It could also be a single event such as a school trip, or it could be a policy, or an area of the school such as a computer room.

Be careful with that last example. Remember that in a case study, you need to secure permission from all participants in the case (Ethics, Chapter 4), so if for example you choose to look at how multiple groups use a room, you would need to ask for permissions from everyone who will use that room during the periods you are observing.

By contrast, action research, as its name suggests, is interventionist. It explores and measures planned intentional change and is often a more long-term enterprise than a case study. For example, one might experiment with a change of routine; or identify whether the use of a resource produces better outcomes. Action research seeks to solve a problem (perhaps school attendance, playground safety, GCSE outcomes, pupil engagement, behaviour management, the gender gap). Data in action research is often quantitative, and comparisons are made between pre- and post-interventions, and sometimes series of repeated interventions.

Should you choose to undertake action research you would still need to identify your parameters in terms of participants or setting, as you would with a case study approach. But as in all research, the more variables inherent in a study, the less valid the study becomes, so in action research it is important to identify and limit the boundaries of what is being looked at and changed.

The Connection Between a Research Design and a Paradigm

The reason that the vast majority of research studies we have supervised on undergraduate teacher training courses and PGCEs have employed a case study approach is because it is highly unlikely that you will have time to undertake anything longer-term. But your case study is not bound within a single paradigm. For example, Cherrelle is interested in the use of role play in Key Stage 3, and she intends to apply this question to her Year 9 History groups who are exploring what it would have been like to be a teenager during the Second World War when the air raid sirens sounded in London, and everyone took shelter in the underground train network. She is a bit undecided, but she thinks she wants to employ a case study approach because she has a university submission deadline and so cannot afford a long action research time frame, but at this early stage in her planning, action research remains an option. She is also still considering the collection of quantitative data as well as qualitative.

Table 3.1 identifies Cherrelle's thinking about how her design and possible title could be directed by the paradigm(s) and research model she chooses, and how the vocabulary of her research question may also be dictated or influenced by these decisions.

Table 3.1 How the Selection of a Paradigm Can Inform a Potential Enquiry Design

	Quantitative Paradigm (Positivist)	Qualitative Paradigm (Interpretivist)
Case study	How often do teachers intervene in children's role play? Which are the most used resources in role play activities?	Teachers' attitudes and priorities when using role play. Children's perceptions of the use of role play.
Action research	Does role play increase the frequency of children's use of subject-based vocabulary?	Can children get better at doing role play over time? What skills need to be taught to improve children's enjoyment and motivation of role play in classrooms?

The second row of Table 3.1 (case study) shows that there is nothing stopping Cherrelle from employing either quantitative or qualitative paradigms (or both) in her case study for her research project. Indeed, such triangulation would strengthen it. If she collects both quantitative and qualitative data, hers can still be a case study because she would be taking a single snapshot of what is happening within specific parameters of focus, time and personnel, even though she is using different approaches within that window. But the action research possibilities are also attractive to her, if only she had more time.

Cherrelle has realised, even before collecting any data, that her choice of design and paradigm will inform the sorts of research question she can ask, and not the other way round. She will go on to make this point clearly in the introduction to her methodology. In time, Cherrelle will decide to go with a case study, but in so doing she will be pleased that she at least considered another possibility, which helped to clarify her thinking.

This realisation on Cherrelle's part goes back to a consideration of the nature of knowledge (Chapter 2).

▬▬▬ Reflective Questions 3.2 ▬▬▬

Is Cherrelle exploring a problem of ignorance or confusion? Is she exploring perceptions? Behaviours? Skills? Facts? Is she counting or categorising? Cherrelle realises (correctly) that if she is to get a good grade, she needs to be sure about what she is trying to find out, and as a corollary, the nature of the data she is trying to collect.

Intrinsic and Instrumental Case Studies: Examples

On reading this chapter so far, you have probably decided that a case study approach is the most appropriate for your research project. If this is the case, in an attempt to impress your marker and enhance your grade, you should also be mindful of what type of case study you are designing. For example, Jack and Rabia are in different schools, both in Key Stage 2, but each has developed an interest in their own use of Learning Support Assistants (LSAs), because this is an aspect of their own professional development which they each find challenging. Jack has designed his study across the school, interviewing as many teachers and LSAs as he can across multiple year groups and across key stages, to get a picture of the variety of ways in which LSAs are utilised, and the relationships that exist between teachers and LSAs. He is hoping to explore the power dynamics at work, and to identify the amount of autonomy LSAs have or want. Jack is doing an *instrumental case study*, in that the selection of specific participants is not fundamental to his question. He wants a cross-section of views. If a particular participant declines to engage with his study, that is not a big problem. He will include as many people as he can cope with, and he might even go to a different school too if necessary. The participants will shed a light on his question, irrespective of who they are, (although they must be Key Stage 2 teachers or LSAs) and Jack understands that since case studies are only a snapshot of a particular identifiable group or situation and therefore not generalisable, his data will be relevant, irrespective of who provides it.

Rabia, by contrast, is captivated by the professional relationship between her host teacher Tom, and Rachel, the LSA for that class. Tom and Rachel seem to work together symbiotically. There is the briefest of brief conversation between them at the start of a day, but Rachel takes an active role in the group teaching and the assessment of the children. Rabia realises that it is not possible in the time that they spend talking at the start of the day that Tom could give Rachel specific instructions for the day, yet they work together like a well-oiled machine. Rachel even involves herself in behaviour management and has more authority within the classroom than any other LSA Rabia has ever seen, and Rabia wants to know more about this compelling relationship. Rabia is planning an *intrinsic case study*, in that she only wants to know about Tom and Rachel. If either of them declines to participate, the study is over before it even starts.

Intrinsic case studies need not be small-scale. One might identify how children and staff move around a particular school or part of a school, which would be a study specific to one physical layout, perhaps at a particular time of day, and only relevant to that one school but would involve a lot of participants.

Rabia's intrinsic case study looks very attractive, but it comes with problems, almost all of them ethical. Rabia is likely to have this study declined by the ethics committee, not because the committee wants to be obstructive, but because studies of very small numbers of people, adults, or children, are ethically high-risk. The participants in Rabia's study would be easily identifiable, and the risk of harm would be great, because Rabia is intending to probe into what looks to her to be a perfect working relationship. And it probably is a perfect working relationship. But wouldn't it be awful if it turned out that the brief conversations Rabia sees in the morning are so short because Tom and Rachel can't stand each other and choose to work independently, each merely tolerating what the other does. Rabia has not considered that when Rachel gets involved with behaviour management, Tom feels this undermines his authority, and it drives him mad. Tom may have deliberately hidden all this from Rabia because as the class teacher, he is a bit ashamed of the situation, and since Rabia is only with them for a term, he does not talk about it with her. In planning her study, Rabia could be unknowingly intending to invite Tom and Rachel to articulate key features of their toxic relationship, the basis of which Rabia is ignorant. On this occasion, the ethics committee is right to remove the risk of Rabia making a bad situation significantly worse.

The ethical problems would be even more pronounced if there were individual children that you wanted to study as a case, because children are vulnerable, and it is likely you would want to involve children of interest, perhaps with physical, behavioural, or cognitive challenges. We strongly advise you against such research for the purposes of an assessed research project.

To return to your own research project, should you choose to undertake a case study, it would enhance the strength of your submission to identify your awareness of instrumental and intrinsic case studies. Many research project submissions that we have read and graded simply state that the student is undertaking a case study, with little or no explanation of what that means, and certainly with no exploration of different types, or the ethical implications that might arise.

━━━━━━━━ **Reflective Questions 3.3** ━━━━━━━━

- What would be the disadvantages and advantages of selecting either a case study or action research for your study?
- If you already think you know what your research project will focus on, can you imagine it as a case study and also as a piece of action research? Which feels more 'right'?
- What is your understanding of generalisability? How big in terms of the number of participants might a study have to be before you could generalise from it?

RESEARCH GENRES

We will now look at different types of research.

Research With Human Participants

It is likely (though by no means certain) that your research project will involve human participants. Indeed, your university, college, or initial teacher training provider may encourage this, because the object of a research project is not only to allow you space to explore a question that interests you, but also to help you learn important aspects of research in education. Research with human participants develops your transferable skills and knowledge of methodologies, ethics and data organisation, but also enhances your professional development. By giving you the opportunity to explore the behaviours or perceptions of children and/or education professionals, your university or college is promoting skills which are clearly relevant to its goals and reputation, and to the teaching qualifications it offers.

If researching with human participants, here is a menu: a list of some typical activities that you might consider asking participants to engage in, and some features or advice on each.

Group Interviews
- Always do group interviews with children, never individual. Apart from the safeguarding issue, group interviews give children confidence to speak, especially if they do not know you well.
- Group interviews are time efficient – a plurality of participants can be involved at the same time.
- They allow participants to hear, support, or challenge different points of view, so everyone benefits from the actual process of data collection.
- They sometimes promote discussion about things that are important to the participants that you had not thought to raise.

- Take care to prevent the most confident from dominating the discussion.
- Consider how you will identify a participant and their data if they choose to withdraw after the discussion.

Individual Interviews

- You may prefer to interview teachers or adult participants individually, simply because arranging diaries for group interviews can prove challenging.
- They allow participants space to think. Thoughtful silences are common. Don't be afraid to allow silence in an interview.
- You are more likely to get a wider range of responses in individual interviews than from a group interview – participants can often feel safe to offer sensitive or individualised responses that would not be shared with a group.

Surveys

- Surveys are good for situations when you have lots of participants, perhaps in different settings. Responses are usually planned to be short (Likert scales, multiple choice questions) and are therefore easily and quickly analysed, but you will get few surprises, because you are controlling what is asked, and limiting how participants can respond.
- You might want to include an invitation for participants to be interviewed about the responses or about the focus of your research question to get more depth.

Questionnaires

- Questionnaires are good for when you want individual responses but have too many participants to interview, so you are looking for more depth than a survey can offer.
- Questionnaires can involve text responses. They are more difficult and time-consuming to analyse than surveys but offer a greater variety of responses.
- It would be an error to use a questionnaire and then to interview participants, because you are likely to get similar data.

Photography (Lots of Ethical Issues Here If You Are Not Careful)

- You might photograph children's work or the results of their efforts to give examples of your observations, but not to explore individual progress;
- You might photograph classroom resources; classroom layout; displays; inclusive physical features of a school.
- Do not, under any circumstance, photograph or film children, even from behind.
- You must ensure there is nothing in the foreground or background that could identify the name of the school or any participant.

Problem-Solving or Sorting Exercises

- These activities help researchers address gaps in knowledge or the problem that requires your attention. The aim is to use participants to find possible solutions or recommendations to a given research question or scenario. This is usually a group and collaborative process and gives the participants a stake in the research. As well as the solutions or products of these exercises, recording the conversations that participants engage in during them can be a rich and illuminating additional source of data.

- Sorting exercises are used to explore participants' opinions that reveal patterns of thought that may not be discovered by interviews or questionnaires. For example, statements may be put in sequential order of importance, or placed in a diamond pattern, most and least significant or agreed at the top or bottom.
- Some participants may prefer this type of data collection method because it is not direct in nature and offers thinking time and space. Participants may feel less than you are looking for a specific or preferred answer or angle as participants might feel in interview questions.

Drawing

- Not all participants are comfortable converting thoughts into speech or the written word and may prefer the medium of drawing to better express their views. Think of the popularity of drawing-based board games for example. Some participants may prefer a visual creative approach to expressing an opinion or dealing with the world.
- Drawing can result in a quick and permanent, easy to access record that can be used to stimulate further questioning.
- Drawing is not age specific. Do not be afraid to ask adults to draw, as well as children of whatever age. But as with all research, be wary of insisting on it. You might offer drawing as an option and be surprised how many adults (and children) take you up on it.
- Drawing does not have to result in a recognisable picture. For example, it could be representative of a collection of memories, or a wish-list.
- It can replace photography as a data collection method. For example, rather than giving children cameras to photograph their favourite resources, features of a school trip, or parts of the school (an innovative method, but it is highly likely other children will appear in the photographs), asking them to draw these things instead gives you the same information without the safeguarding issues.
- Make clear to participants that the quality of the drawing is not the big thing. It is not an exercise in art.

Observation

- Observation is a very common method of case study but as with photography above, it requires careful ethical preparation. This method allows researchers to gather real-time data about human participants and may capture data missed by verbal- or written-based methods.

- With careful use of ethics, observation allows researchers to study participants in their natural environment, for example the classroom or the playground. It allows the interactions between people or objects to be witnessed and recorded.
- Observations also enable researchers to capture non verbal or written data such as body language.
- Observations can be used together with written-based data collection methods to capture more data.
- Observation methods can result in both quantitative and qualitative data. For example, an observation of children's use of a resource might include a description of how they used it, but also an identification of the frequency of use, the number of different children involved, and the time they chose to spend using it.
- Decide whether you are going to be an active, hands-on observer, or a passive, distant one (see observation strategies, Chapter 6).

Diaries

- Diaries tend to be a longer-term method of data collection, but they are useful in capturing on-going and sometimes intimate thoughts from research participants. They can be used daily or weekly and are under the control of the diary writer, without, for example, being in a face-to-face interview that requires answers within a specific period. Diaries can therefore be used in a convenient way for the participant.
- Diaries are reflective and may offer authentic lived experiences of research participants.
- You should not dictate what a diary entry might look like, but participants will need to know and be guided by what your focus is, and what your intentions are (ethics again). You will get richer and more authentic data if you allow participants to keep the diary in whatever style they prefer. Some participants will write in grammatically correct, helpfully paragraphed extended prose. Some will use bullet points. Others will doodle and sketch. Some diaries will be very tidy, whilst others will look a right mess. Some will be in chronological order, whilst others will be structured by themes, events or incidents. Some will contain entries written meticulously regularly on agreed days or times. Some will be completed as and when participants are moved to do so, or something significant happens to remind them. All are useful.
- Some participants will prefer to keep the diary in digital format, whereas others will choose to maintain a hard copy. In our experience, digitally produced diaries provide less insight than those in hard copy, perhaps because it is easier to delete entries, and they also tend to be exclusively in written form.
- In our experience, compared with other data collection methods, amongst studies that contain diaries there is a somewhat higher incidence of participants choosing to withdraw from studies, or to stop halfway through, or to prefer not to share some pages or diary entries. This is because diaries can be quite revealing, even for the

participants themselves. Surprises can be common. Keeping a diary can be a deeply personal thing. You should make clear to participants at the outset that a partial diary is more useful to you than no diary at all, or perhaps having made the diary, participants might prefer to talk to you about them rather than hand them over.

Research Without Human Participants

Not all trainees choose or are able to include human participants. This could be because their interest or focus lies in a question that does not demand it (in which case the decision not to involve human participants should be celebrated, not apologised for). It could also be the result of reasons outside of your control when the logistics of your situation or setting do not allow it. For example, perhaps your school leadership team has, for whatever reason, declined to allow you to seek permissions from parents, or perhaps they are protecting their staff from feeling obliged to take part because the teachers already have very challenging workloads.

It is also the case that instead of analysing primary data (data you have generated and collected yourself) you may choose to analyse secondary data – data that has already been collected by others and is in the public domain. For example, you might mine national statistics, government publications, and data from a range of published sources to interrogate a research question. This could be a useful approach if you were looking to explore a very sensitive area that you are passionate about (for example the experiences of children or teachers with rare or specific difficulties or characteristics) and it would be impossible to get ethical approval for you to collect data from adults or children around those areas.

If your study does not involve human participants, do not be worried. Even though this is not a common approach in research project submissions, you should not think that this is a second-class choice of approach, or it is somehow shameful, or that your chances of getting a good grade are diminished as a result. If, for example, you are exploring key features of behaviour management policies in one or more schools, but without involving human participants, it is true that ethical considerations are greatly reduced, but they are not entirely absent (for example, you would still need an ethics section within your methodology, demonstrating safeguards about institutional ano-nymity, and how you gained permission to report on the policies).

It may even be that you are taking a rather philosophical approach, and your research project takes the form of an extended literature review. For example, you might choose a title such as 'To what extent is the national curriculum (2013) an inclusive document?', or 'Is there a moral imperative to formally educate children?'. These are questions that could involve human participants, or not. If you choose not to, you could still produce a very lively and well-informed literature review for either focus, each with detailed def-initions and parameters. This would be an unusual approach to an assessed research project, but we have known it. Be careful here, though. You would need to first check with your supervisor that such an approach would enable you to satisfy each of the assessment criteria of your module.

Other Examples of Research Questions Where Human Participants May be Unwise or Not Essential

- What are the effects of poverty on attainment in secondary education?
- Why do schools use therapy dogs (and how does it impact children, and the dogs)?
- Do the books in a primary school library reflect the diversity of the children who may read them?
- How are playgrounds designed to maximise children's play?
- A review of curriculum policy.
- Key features of school policies promoting Equality, Diversity and Inclusion.
- Does Bloom's Revised Taxonomy (2001) still have relevance in twenty-first Century schools?
- Is children's ownership and use of mobile phones a threat or an opportunity in modern schools?
- How have schools been impacted by the increase in home schooling since 2020?
- What are the most common effects of domestic violence on secondary-aged children, and what support and guidance is given to schools by Education authorities?
- How can schools identify children who are being groomed to join violent gangs, and what can schools do to prevent it?
- What do curricula and official guidance say about the need to teach children of ages 3–7 about climate change and sustainability? To what extent is this guidance followed?
- Can't, can, should, or must? Exploring different attitudes, practices, and policies regarding people who work in schools wearing religious symbols or clothing in the workplace.
- To what extent is there still a stigma regarding LGBT in schools, and what provisions can be implemented into secondary schools to help prevent homophobic bullying?
- What implications are there for schools following the 2025 high court ruling that 'sex' in the Equality Act 2010 refers to biological sex?
- Do Black Lives Matter? An exploration into the factors affecting the educational outcomes of Black pupils in UK primary schools.

SUMMARY

The main messages we hope you take from this chapter are:

- You should allow your chosen paradigm and research design to inform your choice of research question and identify to your marker how that has happened.
- There is more than one type of case study.
- We have given suggestions and features of common activities that human participants might be asked to engage in.
- Not all research projects will involve human participants.
- We have given examples of research areas that may not require human participation.

━━━━━ **Activity 3.1** ━━━━━

At this stage, you may wish to create a hypothetical research question and demonstrate your understanding of paradigms, case study and action research. Identify a research question (area of interest) and write or discuss with a fellow student your chosen paradigm. For example, 'I have chosen an interpretivist paradigm because…', then repeat with either a case study approach or with an action research approach. If you are selecting an action research approach show a basic action research cycle.

FURTHER READING

Crotty, M. (1998). *The foundations of social research*. London: SAGE. Introduction.
This book links methodology and theory with great clarity and precision, showing students and researchers how to navigate the maze of conflicting terminology.

Grey, D. (2021). *Doing research in the real world*. 5th edn. London: SAGE.
This book helps you build your knowledge of theory and methods and offers straightforward guidance to empower you to make good research decisions and learn best practice, in a step-by-step process.

McNiff, J. (2017). *Action Research: all you need to know*. London: SAGE.
This book gives you all you need to know about action research, why you need to know it and how it can help you become a self-reflective practitioner-researcher. It provides the ideas and frameworks to understand action research, combined with a practical workbook to guide you through the practicalities and complexities of doing action research in your own context.

Thomas, G. (2021). *How to do your case study*. 3rd edn. London: SAGE.
This accessible guide takes you through the process of designing, conducting and writing up a research project using case study methods in a warm and characteristic style.

Thomas, G. (2023). *How to do your research project*. 4th edn. London: SAGE – Chapter 5.
This book provides easy-to-follow advice to navigate every step of your research project, from choosing your research question, deciding on your research design and methodology, collecting and analysing your data, and writing up your finished project.

Wilson, E. (ed.) (2017). *School-based research*. 3rd edn. London: SAGE.
This is a thorough and thoughtful guide to the research process, covering qualitative, quantitative, and mixed research methods. It guides you through research design, data collection and analysis and how to write up your research findings.

4

ETHICS

========= Chapter Aims =========

This chapter will explore:

- Why an ethical approach is important in an assessed research project in school.
- What needs to be included in an ethics application.
- Data protection.
- Research involving sensitive areas.
- Use of children's progress data.
- Disclosure.
- British Ethical Research Association (2024) guidelines.
- Grey areas, and doing the right thing.
- Acceptable use of artificial intelligence (AI) in your research project.
- Plagiarism and academic misconduct.

WHY IS AN ETHICAL APPROACH IMPORTANT IN AN ASSESSED RESEARCH PROJECT IN SCHOOL?

It comes as a surprise to many trainee teachers that they need to give a good deal of thought to ethics when researching in the classroom. After all, for most of their training, trainees have been involved in assessing and observing children. The school openly monitors children's attendance and progress, individually and collectively. Children's progress is tracked, their data collected, collated and reported to parents, governors and Ofsted. Targets are set from these data. The analyses made by the school may be extended to subcategories of children: for example, by gender, ethnicity, those who have free school meals, special needs, or disabilities. All this is common professional practice. The trainee sees and engages in these data collection, analysis and sub-categorisation, all conducted seemingly without the school giving even the briefest consideration for parental permission (and certainly not the children's).

So why then, when all you want to do is see how Year 1 children react to the intro-duction of an interesting resource in the role play area, is your research project module leader requiring you to send letters home to get written permissions from parents or carers, and additionally to get their permission to ask their children if they would like to take part? Why is it that these letters must have accompanying information sheets identifying the parameters of the task, what the data will be used for, and processes for withdrawal should they wish to. Surely, you ask, isn't the intended activity in the role play area is just like any other activity that you have been regularly organising whilst in placement?

Well, no, it isn't just like any other activity. It is entirely different. For three reasons. Firstly, the initialisation of this activity is designed first and foremost to benefit you, the trainee. You are using this activity to secure perhaps 30 credits in the final year of your degree or PGCE. Yes, it is likely the children will enjoy it, and they will probably benefit from it, but if they don't, you still get your 30 credits. Further, the data you are collecting is not being used to track or observe the children for the children's benefit, or at least it is not only being used for that purpose. There is an additional, non-school-based reason for doing this, and to put it bluntly, the parents have a right to know if their children are being used to provide free data for a third-party beneficiary (you) who will share the data with people at a local university (your supervisor, moderation tutors, and external examiner). The findings may even be published (see Chapter 12), also for your benefit. The school has pupils: you have participants. So no, it is not just like any other activity in school at all.

Secondly, your research project is about you demonstrating your understanding of research methods, and ethics is an important aspect of research. You don't get the top grades only by answering your research question (indeed it is perfectly possible to get a very good grade even if your data provides negative results to your question). To get the top grades you must demonstrate your understanding of research vocabulary, principles and methods. Strong processes regarding research ethics go a long way to showing your marker that you have an awareness of, and commitment to, important research principles.

Thirdly, there is a distinction to be made between your identity as a trainee teacher working with children, and your identity as a researcher working with those same children. In both cases you are involved with the same group of children, but your professional identity is different. In your school placement module, you are required to teach the children and any data accrued from your work there is for the children's, parents' and school's benefit. As a result, in that role there is no ethical reason to comply with General Data Protection Regulations (GDPR, see Data Protection, below). By contrast, as soon as your activity steps outside of your school placement module and into your research project module your professional identity changes. It is a subtle, but legally important change of role and significantly, the rules regarding data collection and protection change too.

WHAT NEEDS TO BE INCLUDED IN AN ETHICS APPLICATION?

Your university or college is likely to give you a form to fill in, but you must be specific. For example, when asked about data protection, it is not enough to say, "This research project will conform to the BERA guidelines (2024) and the Data Protection Act (2018)". That is easily said and does not show your understanding. The ethics committee will want to know how those guidelines are satisfied.

A checklist for you will be helpful here. Remember, you must be specific to demonstrate that you have thought everything through. Please do not imagine, however, that your grade will go up for every one of the things on this list that you include. It does not work like that. Think of it like your commitment to getting washed every morning. No one is going to congratulate you for getting it right, because getting it right is something of an expectation. Rather, like washing, for every one of these you miss, your project gets a bit smellier.

Ethics Permission Checklist

As a minimum you must identify the following (not necessarily in this order):

- Your research question(s).
- The type of setting (primary or secondary school, nursery).
- Age of the participants, and your professional relationship with them, if there is one.
- How many participants are you seeking?
- How will participants be selected?
- What will happen if you get more participants than you need or can cope with?
- How will you gain and evidence the voluntary informed consent of school leaders to conduct your research in their school?
- How will you gain and evidence the voluntary informed consent of parents/carers?
- How will you gain and evidence the voluntary informed assent of children (only adults can give consent)?
- What will you be asking the participants to do (interviews, activities, observations, diaries, surveys, group activities…)?
- How much time will each participant spend doing these things?
- Where will the research take place?
- What resources are you using, and who is providing them?
- What protected personal data will you be collecting (keep this to an absolute minimum)?
- How will you maintain anonymity (the school's and the participants')?
- In what format and/or on what devices will the research data be collected?
- Where will the data be stored?
- How will the data be protected? (see next section, below.)
- On what date will the data be destroyed?
- Are there any risks involved in this research, to you or to your participants (physical, psychological, reputational, relational, time pressures, conflicts of interests …)?
- How can participants withdraw from the study, and what will happen to their data if they do?
- By what date can they withdraw?

- If a participant withdraws, how can you identify and separate their data from everyone else's (particularly relevant if you are doing a group activity, for example)?
- Will you report the findings of your research to participants? If so, how? If not, why not?

You should not see this checklist as being an unwelcome hoop to jump through. By considering each of these areas in turn your thoughts will be focused, your research design tightened, and very importantly, you will gain an appreciation of what it will be like to be a participant in your study. You will also be demonstrating to your marker that you have a strong grasp of ethical principles (and thus your grade will be protected).

Data Protection

If you are undertaking research with human participants, it may come as an additional surprise that your research project comes under the terms of General Data Protection Regulations. You are therefore legally obliged to protect the data you collect, particularly any personal data, but GDPR also requires you and your institution to conform to data collection and protection principles. This is why you must get permission from your university to conduct the research before you start, because you will be doing it under your university's name, and your institution wants to protect itself, and you, from the reputational or financial risk of poorly designed research projects which could lead to data breaches, injury, distress (however unintended), or complaints. A strong ethics application would overtly demonstrate your commitment to good research ethics, and it would also show how you have thought through your research design, consciously avoiding poor practice.

Therefore, you must have permission to generate the data you collect, and you must protect the data from its collection to its deletion. For example, if you are collecting electronic data, perhaps digital recordings of interviews, best practice would be to upload those interviews directly onto your university cloud-based storage platform, where it is password protected, and then to delete it from the device you recorded it on (ideally a voice recorder). Very poor and potentially illegal practice would be to record the interviews on your phone and then carry it around with you for the duration of your research project.

Similarly, if you are collecting data in hard copy, then it must be kept safe, as a minimum under lock and key. It would be best to store it securely in the setting where it was collected so you are not carrying it around with you. This sounds overly cautious, but if you had volunteered to participate in a piece of research, giving information about your professional practice, including perhaps deeply-help attitudes and perceptions, would you be happy to have your data left in school unprotected or transported in the researcher's bag on the bus? No, of course not. As a researcher, you are being entrusted with people's stories, opinions, and articulated experiences. Sometimes people will tell you things they have never expressed before, or perhaps were not expecting to articulate. You owe it to them to treat their responses with the utmost respect.

RESEARCH INVOLVING SENSITIVE AREAS

From an ethical point of view, for the purposes of your assessed research project, it is perhaps unwise to explore sensitive areas, however interested you are in them. The risk of harm is too great for an inexperienced researcher who, with all due respect, is likely to lack the sensitivity and procedural awareness needed to conduct such a study ethically. Such areas might include obvious ones such as gender identity, sexuality, ethnicity, disability, physical or cognitive impairment, neurodiversity, and class. Less obvious areas include such things as children's perceptions concerning what and how they are taught, or anything that might encourage them to have critical thoughts about their school or about teachers that never occurred to them to think before you asked them a direct question.

For example, Emanuel is interested to identify perceptions of healthy eating held by KS2 children who have free school meals. This is an innocent-sounding research question, but before you read on, just stop to think whether you can see any dangerous ethical issues inherent in that question. There are several, and three of them are very serious.

Firstly, there is an assumption that the school is giving healthy meals to children. If that is not the case, or it is the children's perception that this is not the case, then Emanuel's study may provoke judgement of the school by pupils and parents. It may be the first time the children have stopped to consider whether the food they are being given by the school is healthy.

Secondly, for Emanuel to explore his question he will presumably select and interview a selection of KS2 children who have free school meals. In so doing, he is adopting an inclusion criterion that to be involved in his study, children must come from backgrounds of officially recognised financial disadvantage.

Thirdly, the children may or may not be aware that they receive free school meals until Emanuel tells them by including them in his study. That may affect their self-esteem and could even affect their relationship with their parents or carers. It may also identify them to other children as having free school meals, which could result in stigma.

Fourthly, how will Emanuel identify the children who have free school meals in order to approach them? Presumably, he would expect the school to tell him who they are. But he is not entitled to this information for the purposes of his research project unless the school has received permission from the parents. GDPR does not allow it. And imagine the letter sent home. It would be an awkward one to write and a difficult one to receive. In effect, Emanuel would be asking each parent for permission to involve their child in a piece of research and telling them that their child had been chosen for invitation to take part because they (the parents) were unable to afford to feed that child. How insensitive is that? It may well be that in Emanuel's role as a classroom practitioner he does already happen to have access to this protected information, which is what sparked his interest in the subject in the first place, but he is not conducting his research project as a classroom practitioner. In this activity, he is a researcher.

Suddenly, with the realisation of these four impediments, Emanuel's innocent-sounding research question is revealed to be a minefield of insensitivity and data protection problems. Armed with these insights, you can now see that there can be strong ethical tensions between your two roles in school when you choose to explore sensitive areas for the purpose of organised or assessed research. Things that are allowed as a teacher can be forbidden as a researcher, because the prime beneficiaries are different.

The pitfalls of researching sensitive areas also explains why your institution insists that you apply for ethical approval. Emanuel's research question was innocently meant, but people would have been hurt in the process of him securing his 30 credits via a question that genuinely interested him. Ethics committees are made up of experienced researchers who will look at your research intentions and approve or disapprove. Given this last scenario, and looking at the checklist above, a member of the ethics committee would not get past Emanuel's first statement (the identification of the research question) before alarm bells started ringing loudly and insistently.

Bearing in mind that you are reading this book because you want to design and write a strong research project which will attract a good grade, I hope you will agree that Emanuel would be best advised to explore a question situated on much safer ground and leave his focus of those who have free school meals to when he has his own class, and he can talk to some of them about it privately without having to report his findings. Perhaps for his research project he might ask 'What perceptions are held by Key Stage 2 children regarding healthy eating' (although even here you will probably already be anticipating some cultural or religious dietary sensitivities which Emanuel would need to be mindful of).

Accessing Progress Data

Similar ethical problems arise if you are wanting to undertake research involving an analysis of children's progress data. For example, Saira has been reading in the education press about the gender disparities between boys' and girls' reading skills in Key Stages 3 and 4. She is interested to know whether the national statistics are representative of the secondary school she is training in, so she is intending to analyse her school's end of Key Stages 3 and 4 data for the last five years to ascertain whether there is or has recently been a gender divide in reading skills in her school, and she is also intending to interview teachers in order to discover their perceptions. Do the teachers recognise any gender imbalance in this school? If so, what might be done about it? If not, why do they think the school is successful in bucking the national trend? Do teachers in the English department hold different views from those in other departments? Saira is delighted with this research idea. Not only is it an interesting and topical question, but through her analysis of her school's quantitative progress data and her qualitative interview data from the teachers she would also be demonstrating obvious triangulation.

But in the light of the previous example with Emanuel, you can probably already see that her proposal should not get through the ethics committee. Saira, in her role as a researcher, is wanting to use progress data that she is not entitled to and without the permission of the people whose data it is. She would need to secure the permission of parents or carers of all pupils from the last five years. The school would not allow her to contact so many parents, and anyway, the chances of securing a high proportion of permissions would be very slim. And even if Saira did ask the school for this progress data without the need to ask the parents, and the school agreed to it, this is not going to enhance Saira's grade in her research project. In terms of getting a good grade, she would do far better to demonstrate in her submission that for ethical reasons she did not even consider asking for progress data to which she is not entitled. This would overtly demonstrate her understanding of ethical aspects of research.

So yes, Saira can explore teachers' perceptions of gender disparities in reading skills within the school she is training in. She can interview the teachers, and should she wish to she can compare the views of teachers of English with those of other departments. She can use national statistics which are in the public domain, but because of General Data Protection Regulations she cannot simply help herself to individual or cohort progress data if she wants to demonstrate best practice in terms of ethics.

In the end, after talking with other students and after a tutorial with her supervisor, the research question Saira chose was 'What perceptions regarding gender disparities in secondary-aged students' reading skills are held by Key Stage, 3 and 4 teachers in a secondary school in North West London?' This was an ethically sound and appropriate research question, through which Saira could still explore the area she was interested in, but she was no longer trying to prove anything by quantitative analysis of unallowable data, which would have cost her a lot of time, and a lot of marks in her assessed grade. She could still explore whether the national statistics were outworked in her secondary school, but not by number crunching. Instead, she could present the national statistics to her teacher participants, and ask them whether they recognise the proportions of disparity in their own school, and explore with them any of the school's relevant policies, processes and procedures. This softer approach to her research question is strong in terms of an assessed research project because when it comes to exploring and analysing situations or phenomena that involve humans, it makes sense that the voices and perceptions that are held by people whose lives are immersed in those fields are just as valid as hard facts, and are likely to be much more insightful. Saira's participants were much more immediate and nuanced judges of any gender disparity than five years' worth of progress data. Saira realised that because her participants were working with the children, day in and day out, their lived experiences were much more valid and insightful than any number of statistics. She had initially been seduced into thinking that there was safety in the analysis of numbers, when in fact, the opposite is true. It was not only the case that her original number-crunching idea was ethically suspect. Additionally, Saira felt she was far better identifying the perceptions of teachers, many of whom were at the immediate forefront of teaching reading skills, than looking at the question from afar, viewed through the potentially distorting lens of cold numbers.

Disclosure

You will have received mandatory safeguarding training as part of your Initial Teacher Training course, so you will already know about the need to tell children that there are circumstances in which confidentiality must be broken if they disclose things that affect them that are illegal or harmful. The potential for unexpected disclosure can be heightened in research situations if you are not careful. Children may feel safe to disclose things to you, precisely because they are in a research situation, not a usual 'school' one, and so may disclose on the misunderstanding that what they say would go no further. After all, you did make a big thing about the guarantee of anonymity in your information to participants.

In research situations, however, there are ethical tensions here. A trainee may feel they have done an important and good thing if a child discloses in the process of participating in the trainee's research that they are vulnerable or are being abused, threatened or neglected. Consequently, the trainee may feel they have done a service to the child if this is reported. But equally, if that disclosure presents itself directly because of the nature of the child's participation in the research, questions must be asked about the appropriateness of the activities in the study, particularly if you have chosen to ask leading questions.

For example, returning to Emanuel with his exploration of Key Stage 2 children's perceptions regarding healthy eating, he is fairly safe to ask a cohort of children what they think makes a healthy breakfast, but if instead he asks them what they usually have for breakfast, it is highly likely that at least one of them will tell him that they do not have breakfast, or that they come to school hungry, or that breakfast is made up of foodstuffs that Emanuel considers to be inadequate or very unhealthy indeed. There are two problems here, the first ethical, and the second procedural. Firstly, from an ethics point of view, Emanuel has walked straight into a potential well-being situation of his own making in which he unthinkingly yet directly invited a child to disclose private information and now he must decide whether to share this information with someone in the school. As a result, Emanuel is no longer just a researcher. He has inadvertently and unwillingly become a preliminary arm of social services. Secondly and procedurally, his question to the children is irrelevant to his research question, and so will not contribute to his research project at all. He has promised to explore perceptions of healthy eating, not to catalogue what children eat. The child who eats no breakfast or has a range of sweets and biscuits may have strong and compelling views on what constitutes a healthy breakfast, irrespective of what they eat or are given in the morning, and irrespective of how these perceptions align to Emanuel's views about what a healthy breakfast should contain.

This is not to say that if during a research project a child discloses worrying information, you should not share it within the processes and procedures of the school. Of course you should, if it was spontaneously disclosed. But equally you should not be thoughtlessly fishing for such information either. In your safeguarding training will have learnt that a referral could be compromised if you had secured information by asking leading questions. For your research project, you are therefore advised not to choose research questions or data collection tools that are likely to produce highly personal responses. Because of thoughtlessness, Emanuel very easily slipped into an irrelevant yet compromising choice of interview question. You should ensure that if you choose to interview or survey children, the questions you ask will generate responses that lead directly to a consideration of your research focus. If you are exploring perceptions, do not make the mistake of asking about specific behaviours of participants.

British Educational Research Association (BERA)

A very high proportion of trainees that we have supervised and supported are aware of BERA. Trainees confidently cite the latest guidance on ethical research (BERA, 2024), but it must be said that in our view, few trainees have taken the trouble to read it. The guidance contains 83 recommendations, spread across five areas, which are:

- *Responsibilities to participants* (49 guidelines).
- *Responsibilities to sponsors, clients, stakeholders and the environment* (8 guidelines).
- *Responsibilities to the community of educational researchers* (12 guidelines).
- *Responsibilities for publication and dissemination* (12 guidelines).
- *Responsibilities for researchers' well-being and development* (2 guidelines).

(BERA, 2024: 9–10)

Under *Responsibilities to Participants,* the guidance explores first principles; consent; transparency; the right to withdraw; incentives; harm arising from participation; privacy and data storage; and disclosure, all of which have been explored and emphasised in this chapter. If you were to cite specific guidance numbers in your ethics application, and if you were to identify within your submission specific aspects of the guidance which informed the design of your study; or which were more challenging than others to satisfy; or which did more than any other to safeguard your participants (or yourself), this would be a very strong thing to do. Your marker would almost certainly notice, and your grade would become upwardly mobile again as a result.

Grey Areas and Doing the Right Thing

It is highly likely that when doing your research project, you will experience a situation in which you wonder whether a course of action is the right thing to do. Because you are inexperienced you may not be able to tell the difference between what is a grey area, and what is just wrong. If in doubt, always ask your supervisor before the event, rather than after, if you can. If that is not possible, acknowledge what happened. Do not hide things because you are unsure.

Here are eight quite common scenarios. Consider why these scenarios would offer an ethical challenge to your study. Reference to the identified BERA (2024) guidelines will identify good practice to you in these examples.

1 You were intending to interview three Year 8 pupils at break time and only one turns up. This places you in a vulnerable situation. Should you continue? (BERA, 2024: guideline 82).
2 A Year 3 girl, whose English is not her first language, struggles to find the words to articulate her experiences about yesterday's school trip to a local museum, but she

really enjoyed the trip, and has much she wants to say about what she learnt and did. You are certain you understand what she is rather stiltedly trying to say, and it is good stuff – highly relevant to your study about kinaesthetic aspects of learning, so when producing the transcripts, you write what she almost certainly meant, not what she actually said (BERA, 2024: guideline 75).

3 Using Likert scales, your quantitative survey data on Year 7 boys' attitudes to doing dance in PE (61 participants) shows pleasingly consistent patterns from most of them, but five boys' data rather contradict the rest. You even wonder whether one of these five was paying attention at all. Since these five boys constitute fewer than 10% of the sample, you consider it unhelpful to report their views, because they are clearly not representative of the cohort (BERA, 2024: guideline 69).

4 For purposes of individualised learning, a Key Stage 3 music teacher is really interested in the children's individual responses about current or historical musicians who the children admire or consider culturally influential, and she wonders whether you would share the data with her once you have finished with it (BERA, 2024: guideline 46).

5 You want to interview KS2 teachers about their use of IT, but everyone is so busy. You are not getting enough participants, and time is running out. You think that offering participants vouchers for the nearby shopping centre is probably not allowed because that would count as an incentive, and you cannot afford that anyway, but surely it would be OK to offer to do additional playtime duties for them, or an assembly or two, in return for their participation, and to free them up a bit (BERA, 2024: guideline 33).

6 A Key Stage 4 teacher in the Art and Design department, when asked about which resources he finds most useful, is scathing about the department's budget. "How on earth are we expected to get good GCSE results if they don't fund consumables?" Given that your title is about teachers' perceptions, do you report that response, which is openly critical of the school? (BERA, 2024: guidance 43).

7 You have arranged for the children in your reception class to do some mark making on the outdoor tarmac area using paint brushes and buckets of water, while you observe, take notes, and photograph their marks (you are very careful not to photograph the children). Four children, Paul, Zhiyu, Luna, and Jacob, are enthusiastically taking part, and now Amelia wants to join in. But unlike the four, a permission slip to take part in your study has not been returned from Amelia's parents. Surely, you decide, it would be cruel to turn Amelia away, so you let her join in, but you do not make notes or collect any data on what she is doing (BERA, 2024: guidance 16).

8 You are exploring how Key Stage 4 students make decisions about further study or career options. The cohort of participants suggest that rather than doing group interviews or surveys, they would prefer to engage with your study through a WhatsApp group. They argue that this would serve as a convenient asynchronous data collection tool meaning it would not take up time at school. You are tempted

by this as you could analyse the data more easily, knowing exactly who had said what; it would save you the task of transcribing interview responses; and the likelihood is that since the students suggested it, it would increase engagement in your study (BERA, 2024: guidance 39 and 44).

If any of these situations arise (and it is very likely that at least one will), acknowledge and report it in your research project, and identify how you dealt with it following your engagement with the BERA guidelines (2024) and with your supervisor. Again, this will demonstrate your commitment to best practice, and potentially enhance your grade.

ACCEPTABLE USE OF AI IN YOUR RESEARCH PROJECT

The unethical use of AI is a huge challenge to universities, the most obvious example being the production of AI-generated essays on demand, but this is not to say that universities consider AI to be, by default, a Bad Thing. All universities have now developed policies on the use of AI, and most have a recommended or preferred AI assistant, and have identified situations or research practices where the use of AI is not only tolerated, it is often encouraged. Our own university recommends Microsoft's Copilot, but there are other AI assistants. One area in which universities actively encourage AI use is its use as a learning aid such as finding materials on a topic which you then go on to consider in more depth. For your research project this might include asking an AI assistant for the main themes, writers, publications or arguments surrounding your research project title, or even asking for suggested titles within a given research area. This gives you the confidence to then go on to explore those areas, knowing that you are unlikely to be missing any large and important aspects of your field.

Similarly, regarding your research method design, you could ask the AI assistant to suggest questions you might include in a survey, questionnaire, or interview to explore your research question. Here you are entering the field of generative AI, which is where problems can arise if you are not careful and transparent. This is not to say your institution would penalise you if you were to generate questions in this way, but you should acknowledge it, and you should also ask yourself whether the questions could be phrased differently to suit your specific participants, or whether to use the questions at all. You should not unthinkingly ask only the questions that AI has suggested. We would hope that you would want to take responsible ownership of what happens in your research project by tailoring those AI-generated questions to your own purposes, rejecting some, adapting others, and adding more to make them specific to your setting. Please remember that AI is your assistant, not your source. You would still need to identify in your methodology why you (yes, you, not an algorithm) have chosen those questions, both in terms of their content and type, but such use of generative AI gives you a very good first step, which your university will encourage. An AI assistant should save you time, help you search, and give you suggestions, and in so doing those things its use is entirely ethical. Where it becomes unethical is if you allow AI to do your thinking for you.

In this regard, you must be particularly on your guard for what is termed 'hallucination', which occurs when AI generates responses that appear plausible, but are factually incorrect. You would be surprised how common this is. Remember that your marker is likely to be very much more experienced than you in all things educational, and statements and statistics that probably sound right to you, may not to them. Be prepared to be challenged on anything that is in your submission.

You will need to make a declaration about how you have used AI, particularly for generative AI. Universities may vary in how they require you to do this, so you should check the guidance of your institution. For your research project, as a minimum you must reference all types of material that you have asked AI to generate, and your university will provide guidelines on how you should do this. This would include text, images, code, and even ideas.

A specific example of how one student, Ashley, successfully and ethically used AI is given in Chapter 7.

You may be using AI such as ChatGPT, Paperpal, QuillBot, Wordtune, Writesonic, STORM, Zetero, Menderley, Scolarcy, Authorea, and DeepSeek to help you with your writing. Do check with your university regulations about using these. It could be that your university policy on using AI would remind students that submitting text generated by AI as your own work is an academic offence and doing so will incur strict penalties.

That said, we are not opposing the use of AI if used responsibly and with integrity; it is beneficial with the immediate caveat that the originality of thought must be your own. You need to acknowledge any use of generative AI output in your work. You should provide a full and proper citation and reference list entry where possible. Anything that is not your own original creation or thoughts should be appropriately referenced with the name of the AI technology used.

This is the response ChatGPT gave us when we asked it to post a warning about the use of ChatGPT in academic dissertations:

'While AI tools such as ChatGPT, grammar checkers, and translation software can be useful for generating ideas, structuring your thoughts, or improving clarity, they must be used with extreme care in your dissertation. Copying AI-generated text and presenting it as your own is plagiarism, even if no human wrote it, and can lead to academic misconduct penalties. AI can also produce inaccurate information, fabricated references, and a writing style that does not match your own, which examiners will notice. Most importantly, your dissertation is an assessment of your independent research and critical thinking – AI cannot replace these skills. If you choose to use AI, follow your university's guidance, avoid inputting any personal or sensitive data, and be prepared to explain how it supported (but did not replace) your own work'. (ChatGPT; August 2025).

You can use AI (and we would suggest that it is helpful to do so) for the following: gathering ideas, checking the meanings of terms, rephrasing the occasional sentence to improve its flow or to enhance its meaning (but rarely). It is not to be used for generating text or analysing data. Please do not use AI to generate references that are false. We have noticed a rise in the number of students doing this and it has led to plagiarism penalties being applied. There is AI technology that will find references as you type in text of your own creation – but seek your university advice about how these can be utilised.

ACADEMIC MISCONDUCT, INCLUDING PLAGIARISM

Everyone knows that plagiarism is wrong, but not everyone is clear about what plagiarism is, and what it is not. Plagiarism can be intentional or unintentional, and from our experience it usually tends to be the latter. It is quite rare for students to be brazen enough to choose to actively plagiarise. This is why a significant proportion of students who have been taken to plagiarism panels had no prior idea that what they were being accused of was not allowed. Obviously, cutting and pasting published work without both acknowledgement and the use of quotation marks is plagiarism (some would say theft, and we would agree with them). The same is true of copying from the work of other students (not as rare as you might think). But academic misconduct, of which plagiarism is the most famous component, is a broad area, and so we briefly explore here things that your university will, and will not, consider under the umbrella of misconduct.

This chapter will now explore and explain the following scenarios. Before you read on, please consider which of these you think might be considered academic misconduct, and which might not.

- Collaboration: students sharing similar research questions discussing and planning a way or ways to go about exploring it or jointly searching for literature.
- Collusion (or is this still collaboration?): students doing all the above, and also planning the detailed structure of their chapters, including subheadings.
- Collusion: students doing all the above, and together writing and submitting virtually identical research projects, just with different vocabulary or sentence order to try to avoid detection from Turnitin.
- Manipulation: taking published work and systematically rewriting it, sentence by sentence, changing all the key words using synonyms as you go along.
- Using AI tools to identify main themes and arguments.
- Copying the method of other research studies.
- Collecting data from human participants without having secured ethical approval.
- Ignoring the advice of your supervisor.

Collaboration

Florence and Nikita were conducting their final teaching placement in different secondary schools. They had the same research project interest (What differences of priority and practice are there between the way PE teachers in Key stages 3 and 4 undertake indoor and outdoor lessons?). In the planning stages of their projects, these two students talked regularly about how their research question might be framed, what sorts of interview questions they might ask teachers, what areas they might include in the interviews (resources, safety, planning, assessment, use of voice, progression) and whether they would incorporate observations. They both thought that a comparison of the actual plans that teachers were working from would be helpful. They shared with each other the literature they had each found and discussed how the various readings cohered or diverged. They even talked about their individual tutorials with their supervisor (who, for both of them, unsurprisingly, was the university's PE tutor, Janet). The supervisor realised their titles were very similar, and on finding they were initially discussing their plans, at an early stage counselled them to be sure to only collaborate, but not to collude.

There is nothing wrong with any of what Florence or Nikita (or Janet) have done in terms of academic integrity, indeed, it might even be encouraged. The benefits of talk in the learning process, and the sharing of ideas and discussing reasons to accept or reject them are well known. Having planned their similar projects, Florence and Nikita went away and read their shared selection of sources. They wrote their literature reviews independently. It is true their methodologies were very similar, but again, they were individually written and presented. Florence and Nikita's submissions were very much stronger because of this early collaboration. They had had opportunities to discuss things in depth with another interested party, but they had done nothing wrong. Collaboration is not plagiarism.

Where Collaboration and Collusion Meet

Things would have started to become messy in terms of plagiarism if Florence and Nikita had taken their research relationship any further, and sometimes this can be hard to avoid, so you must be very careful. Collusion occurs when two or more people secretly do or plan to do something, usually for deceitful or unethical purposes. Imagine if Florence was academically much weaker than Nikita, and she (Florence) was having trouble making sense of what she was reading and in structuring her literature review. Perhaps she is at a loss to know what the main themes or subheadings might be. An obvious first point of call for her might be Nikita, who it turns out has already made great strides in her work, has a clear sense of organisation and direction, and has her subheadings decided and written in draft already. What is Nikita to do? It would be highly awkward for Nikita to tell Florence that she was unwilling to help, since up to this point, they had been something of a team. But if she does help, suddenly Florence's work is no longer entirely her own. And where will it stop? Will Florence later also want help from Nikita with data analysis? Might Florence actually ask for sight of Nikita's data, since the data Florence has collected is a bit thin or disorganised? You can see how easily collaboration can start to become collusion. Through no fault of her own, Nikita is being sucked into a situation she feels unable to control, and for which they could both be penalised, since both students' written submissions become more and more similar. So be strongly advised. It is essential that if you choose to collaborate with another student in the planning stages of your work, you must make an agreement not to liaise with each other during the writing stage, and you must stick to that agreement. That way, Nikita can politely remind Florence of their agreement, and the awkwardness is at least reduced. Also, and more importantly, Nikita is spared being placed in a compromising position.

Collusion

Had Florence and Nikita agreed to plan their literature review in a detailed way, with identical subheadings, identical arguments, made in the same order, citing the same people, coming to the same conclusions, their work would have been virtually indistinguishable. That is blatant collusion and is a clear example of academic misconduct, for which both are liable to be penalised.

Manipulation

Clara, a secondary history trainee, has found an article (Javornik, Š. & Klemencic Mirazchiyski, E. (2023) 'Factors Contributing to School Effectiveness: A Systematic Literature Review' *European Journal of Investigation in Health, Psychology and Education* Vol 13, pp 2095–2111) that perfectly encapsulates her research question about the difference in perceptions teachers hold about what constitutes pupil achievement (her title was 'To what extent are teachers' understandings of pupil achievement confined to pupils' academic achievements?'). To this end, Clara took Javornik & Klemencic Mirazchiyski's literature review and discussion, cut and pasted 2000 words of it into her research project and then spent a day and a half systematically going through it, changing the key words one by one, sentence by sentence. For example, she changed 'There seems to be a lack of consensus among researchers regarding the similarities and differences among the constructs of academic performance, achievement, and learning outcomes, and academic achievement should be considered as multifaceted ... comprising different domains of learning' to 'There is little agreement in published literature concerning definitions of academic performance, academic achievement and how these relate to learning outcomes, because academic achievement is multi-dimensional, made up as it is of a plurality of facets and factors'. Clara carried on in this way for the full 2000 words. She manipulated the subheadings that had been used by Javornik & Klemencic Mirazchiyski, and used them in the same order (for example, Clara used 'Social and Demographic Factors' as a subheading instead of Javornik & Klemencic Mirazchiyski's 'Sociodemographic Characteristics'). Clara quoted the citations that they quoted, and in the same order. The names Javornik & Klemencic Mirazchiyski did not appear anywhere in Clara's work, or in her bibliography. Clara assumed that since she had changed just about everything, it had become her work, not Javornik & Klemencic Mirazchiyski's. In this, Clara was wrong.

Things got worse for Clara when in the plagiarism panel she argued that since what she had written was not the same as what Javornik & Klemencic Mirazchiyski (2023) had written, it could not be plagiarism. She denied having done anything wrong and was adamant about this. She argued that Javornik & Klemencic Mirazchiyski had not even used most of the words that she had used, so how could this be plagiarism? Clara displayed a clear lack of understanding about what constitutes cutting and pasting. Please be advised that manipulation of text is plagiarism. A penalty percentage deduction was applied to Clara's grade, a plagiarism breach was entered on her record, and Clara was warned about her future conduct.

Using AI Tools to Identify Main Themes and Arguments

This falls into a grey area. Most universities are actively seeking to identify ways in which students can use artificial intelligence ethically and many have a favoured AI tool such as Copilot. Increasingly the use of AI for the discovery of the broad issues within a field is being considered as acceptable, but you should check with your supervisor and your institution's policy on AI use. Generic use of AI for such things as looking for names or sources or for listing the key arguments in a field are allowed, but the use of generative AI to write all or some of your research projects is obviously prohibited.

Copying the Research Method of Other Studies

This is not plagiarism. There are only so many methods a student might choose from for a given research question, and if you find a method that other students or a published author has used, that is fine. In the latter case it would best to state openly in the introduction to your methodology that "The method employed by this study was heavily informed by McArthur (2021) ...", and if you then go on to acknowledge what aspects of McArthur's work you have chosen to recreate, all is well. Academic literature contains very many examples of one researcher recreating the method of another, perhaps in a different setting or with a different research focus. If it is acknowledged, nobody minds.

Collecting Data From Human Participants Without Having Secured Ethical Approval

Although this is not plagiarism, it is academic misconduct, and the same penalties apply. Perhaps your first ethics application was unsuccessful, and you are waiting for a decision for your resubmission, which you are confident will be accepted because you have responded to the panel's feedback. The delay has put you behind schedule, so in order not to waste any more time, although you might not actually collect any data yet, you carry on with recruiting your participants regardless. This is academic misconduct. You cannot engage with participants at all without ethics approval, to the extent that you must not even approach potential participants to recruit or inform them about your study.

Ignoring the Advice of Your Supervisor

This is extremely unwise, but it is not academic misconduct. We have known several students who, on being given advice regarding commended changes to their research project (usually about methods or the extent to which they can claim findings from the data), continue to carry on with their first ideas. Do remember that it is likely that your supervisor will be involved in grading your work. They will not be vindictive in the grade they award just because you chose to ignore their advice, but they do have to grade against set criteria. The advice they gave you would have been given because they considered your original idea to contain weaknesses, omissions or insufficiencies. It makes no sense to ignore the advice of your supervisor and marker, but it is not academic misconduct.

SUMMARY

The big messages we hope you take from this chapter are as follows:

- School data and education research data must be treated, collected, and protected very differently because the primary beneficiaries are different people.
- It is not enough to promise to "do no harm". You must identify how you are ensuring that the risk of harm is minimised across a range of aspects of your study.
- Close attention to research ethics will strengthen your research design.
- An identification of your understanding of research ethics principles together with a demonstration of how they are outworked in your study is highly likely to enhance your grade in an assessed research project.
- Research ethics are not a hoop to jump through, but an important safeguard against unintentional poor practice.
- When protecting your participants you are also protecting yourself, the school, and your university or college.
- When challenges arise, Research Ethics are rarely binary, but you can be confident in doing the right thing (or avoiding doing the wrong thing, which is more important), by applying the BERA guidelines (2024), liaising with your supervisor, and by putting yourself in your participants' position when deciding what to do in any potentially compromising situation. Honest articulation within the text of your research project regarding the challenges you experienced, together with your informed response to them, will enhance your grade.
- If you are particularly passionate about aspects of your chosen research question, this can jeopardise your ability to undertake your research in a neutral and balanced way, and can easily lead to ethical or methodological problems if you are not careful.
- If you are particularly passionate about a subject or an ideology, and this is incorporated into your research project, it can be difficult to take a neutral stance. This can skew your reading, method and/or your data analysis if you are not careful.
- The use of AI within acceptable and identified parameters is encouraged by most UK universities. You should, however, be especially transparent about your use of generative AI.
- We have identified aspects of academic misconduct beyond the obvious plagiarism of cutting and pasting.

FURTHER READING

Alderson, P. and Morrow, V. (2020). *The ethics of research with children and young people: A practical handbook*. 2nd edn. London: SAGE.

This practical handbook examines the ethical questions that arise at each stage of research, from first plans to dissemination and impact. Illustrated with case studies from international and inter-disciplinary research, it offers advice for addressing each ethical question, issue or uncertainty.

British Educational Research Association. (2024). *Ethical guidelines for education research*. 5th edn. London: BERA. [Online]. Available at: https://www.bera.ac.uk/publication/ethical-guidelines-for-educational-research-fifth-edition-2024-onlinehttps://www.bera.ac.uk/publication/ethical-guidelines-for-educational-research-fifth-edition-2024-online

The intended audience for these guidelines is anyone undertaking educational research – whether their job description includes research, or they conduct research within the field (for example, while studying for a qualification or with the intention of improving practice). This includes both independent researchers and practitioners based in educational institutions of any kind.

Brooks, R. te Riele, K. and Maguire, M. (2014). *Ethics and education research*. London: SAGE.

This book specifically focuses on the ethics of Education research. Drawn from the authors' experiences in the UK, Australia, and mainland Europe and with contributions from across the globe, this clear and accessible book includes a wide range of examples.

REFERENCES

Data Protection Act. (2018, c.12). Available at: https://www.legislation.gov.uk/ukpga/2018/12/contents. Accessed December 11, 2025.

McArthur, J., Blackie, M., Pitterson, N., & Rosewell, K. (2021). 'Can and should assessment nurture an orientation to society and social justice?' *Centre for Global Higher Education*, University of Oxford.

5

CHOOSING THE FOCUS AND TITLE OF YOUR RESEARCH

━━━━━━━━━━ Chapter Aims ━━━━━━━━━━

- What might a research project explore?
- Formulating a research question.
- Deciding on how to explore your question.
- Research questions that should be avoided.

INTRODUCTION

For many students, the most daunting aspect of a research project is deciding what to focus on in the first place. It is possible that on discovering that a research project was part of your course, you immediately had an idea about what you would like to focus on, and even which research question(s) you would like to ask, but this is rare. But even if this is the case for you, please do not skip this chapter. Students who, at the very beginning of their research project, have a clear and formulated idea of what they want to study and how they will accomplish it are often quite rigid in their thinking. Consequently, they can fall into unforeseen traps when a bit of flexibility would have allowed them to navigate a different and safer path.

It is more likely however that although you are intrigued by the thought of a research project, and you welcome it, you are unsure where it might take you. Perhaps you have some loose unformulated ideas, but you don't know whether they are good ones or not. There are so many things going on in a school or classroom, you do not know where to start. It is as if you are looking at a menu where you must choose something, but everything (or worse, nothing) compellingly appeals.

This chapter is designed to help you with that initial decision and to formulate a focus. We give examples of the sorts of areas or fields that students commonly focus on, and we identify helpful and unhelpful features that your research question might contain.

Please note, we have used the words 'helpful and unhelpful', not 'good and bad'. 'Good and bad' are adjectives that are too binary to describe a research question. Your research question is likely to evolve over the course of your research project. That is very common and is positive. A helpful question gives you a clear sense of overall direction but does not dictate what the outcomes might be. An unhelpful question is either too broad to be manageable, or so prescriptive and closed that it allows no light in.

WHAT MIGHT YOU EXPLORE?

First and foremost, you should explore something that either interests you a lot, or something that will inform your professional development, or both. It is a good idea to decide upon a field (or general area) before being specific about an actual research question. To help you decide, the following is, in effect, a menu containing common fields explored by research projects we have supervised, but this is not an exhaustive list. There are no poor choices on this menu.

Classroom Management

- Routines.
- Desk layouts.
- Resources.
- Kinaesthetic aspects of learning.
- Timings.

Behaviour Management

- Routines, strategies, and/or resources.
- Policies.
- Whole-class and small-group strategies.
- Key Stage specific strategies.
- Restorative justice.

Subject-Focused

- Teachers' priorities in teaching a particular subject.
- Impact of the National Curriculum.
- Cross-curriculum teaching.
- Resource use.
- Prioritisation of STEM subjects.
- Planning.

Planning

- Policies.
- Long/medium/short-term planning.
- Planning for an event.

Transitions

- Between Key Stages; between schools.

Assessment

- Types (formative, summative, ipsative).
- Assessment for Learning.
- Comparisons between subjects.
- Pupil involvement.

Professional Relationships

- Learning Support Assistants.
- Subject coordination.
- Co-teaching.
- External agencies.

Boys' and/or Girls' Attitudes to

- Dance.
- Science.
- STEM subjects.
- Performance activities.
- Rote learning.
- Learning identities.
- Shared gender spaces.
- Behaviour management.
- Sex education.
- Career aspirations.

Personalised Learning and Adaptive Teaching

- Teachers' strategies.
- Policies.
- Hard to reach children.
- Policies.

Evaluating an Event

- A school trip.
- A school concert.

- A visiting theatre company.
- Changes in school/classroom environment.
- Policy changes.
- An Ofsted inspection.

The School Environment

- Use of a specialist room.
- Displays.
- The playground.
- The pupil voice (e.g., School councils, class captains, ambassadors).

The possibilities are endless, but the process of selecting your field and in so doing filtering your thoughts about what to research will pay you a lot of dividends later.

━━━━━━━━━━ Reflective Questions 5.1 ━━━━━━━━━━

- What motivates you as a trainee teacher, and should/how can this passion inform your choice of research focus?
- Is there a need for research in your school or in your own professional development?
- What contribution to research would you like to make?
- How much scope would you anticipate giving to your research in terms of time, resources and access to the number of participants?
- How much do you already know about your likely research area?

FORMULATING A RESEARCH QUESTION

Once you have decided on a field that attracts you, you can start to formulate the title of your research project. Remember, this can evolve as you go along, and that is common. You may be surprised that consideration of the formulation of your research question comes in Chapter 5 of this book, not Chapter 1, but if that reaction on your part is the case, and you have now applied the groundwork steps contained in previous chapters to your thinking, you will have probably improved the grade of your project by about 10%–20% already.

Joshua has decided to explore adaptive teaching, which is an area of his professional practice that he has long struggled with. His research project tutor has told him to try to be specific in his title, so that he can identify clear parameters and limit the scope that his literature review must cover. His first attempt at formulating a title is "Adaptive teaching across the curriculum", which he thinks is a bit vague, but it is better than "Adaptive teaching" which was his first thought.

━━━━━━━━━ **Reflective Questions 5.2** ━━━━━━━━━

Pause in your reading to consider what advice Joshua's supervisor might give him on reading his intended title. You are probably (and rightly) quite critical of it already, but why? How might it be improved?

Well, to some extent it is clear what general field Joshua is trying to focus on, but as a title, it is very weak. Firstly, his title is a statement, and that in itself is unhelpful. You will find it much easier to focus your thoughts about what you are trying to research if you can pose your title as a question, because questions can be answered, at least partially, and it is much easier to identify the extent to which you have been successful in your intentions through a question than through a statement. Secondly, there are far too many unidentified aspects in Joshua's title for it to be useful to him in getting the high grades he wants in his research project submission.

For example, which key stage(s) is he focusing on? At present, it is impossible for anyone to tell whether he is a primary trainee seeking to explore adaptive teaching across the whole primary curriculum, or a secondary trainee researching aspects of a subject-based curriculum. Secondly, it is not clear what are the needs of the children he is seeking to adapt his teaching to. As it happens, Joshua wants to find different strategies across Key Stages 3 and 4, but currently, that is not clear. His question could accommodate (for example) differences in ability; age; physical need; curriculum content; or English language proficiency. Joshua is not specific about any of this, because he has not yet thought through what he is trying to achieve. If he submitted a project under his original title, his literature review would have to cover all things adaptive, because his focus is so broad. It would be broad, but very shallow, and therefore unimpressive and unhelpful to his data analysis.

Joshua is a trainee secondary English teacher, and he is blithely assuming that his supervisor will know this when reading his proposal and would therefore also know what Joshua's intentions are. He is forgetting that his submission will be anonymously blind second marked. If Joshua wants a good grade, it is a very dangerous thing to do to assume that his markers will recognise him from his work, and will know or assume things about him, or about his subject. Joshua must consistently demonstrate his knowledge, not assume the knowledge of his marker(s).

In a tutorial with his supervisor, Joshua is helped to narrow his title bit by bit, and it gets stronger with each iteration. There are any number of possibilities in the direction in which his research might ultimately go. We explore several here.

Outcome Possibility 1

→ Adaptive teaching across the curriculum (this is a statement, so it is unhelpful).
→ Adaptive teaching across the English curriculum.
→ Adaptive teaching across the secondary English curriculum (still a statement).
→ What differences are there between the ways teachers of English adapt their teaching in Key Stage 3 and in Key Stage 4? (A question – good. We are getting there)

→ What factors inform differences in the ways teachers of English adapt their teaching for learners in Key Stages 3 and 4?

Joshua is beginning to get to a sufficiently specific title, formulated as a question, but he is not there yet. He is now much more specific than when he began, but if he submits work under this last title, it appears that he is intending to generalise about how all Key Stages 3 and 4 teachers of English everywhere adapt their teaching. Obviously, that is not Joshua's intention, but that is how it currently reads. He still has work to do on his question, and his supervisor must therefore make him more specific still.

→ What factors inform differences in the ways teachers of English in a secondary school in Greater Manchester adapt their teaching for learners in Key Stages 3 and 4?

Now he has a manageable research question. He could make it even more specific, perhaps if his participants talk in an unprovoked way about specific things such as gender or disability, but for now both he and his supervisor are happy that he has a working title. Joshua, who is doing his teacher training placement in Rochdale, is no longer promising to discover and condense the combined experiences of teachers of English everywhere. He is merely collating the experiences, preferences and perceptions of a small selection of teachers in a school he has access to in Rochdale, and reporting them in an organised form, whilst identifying the extent to which they align (or do not) with the literature he has found which speaks of adaptive teaching generally, and adaptive teaching in English in particular. He has not found any literature which focuses on the differences in adaptation of English teaching between Key Stages 3 and 4 specifically, but his supervisor has assured him this is OK. Joshua wonders, since this is a gap in the literature, and if he gets a good enough grade, he and his tutor might consider publishing an article together (Chapter 12), but let's not run before we can walk.

Joshua feels so much better after his tutorial. He now realises why the title 'Adaptive teaching across the curriculum' was inadequate and unhelpful to a marker, even though, in Joshua's head, the title was always about English teaching in secondary schools. He is so relieved that he does not have to conduct a research project on a grandiose scale. Small and specific is the agreed way forward for him.

Note how Joshua uses 'Greater Manchester' and not 'Rochdale' in his research question to ensure the school's anonymity.

But Joshua's tutorial could have gone in any number of different directions, each with just as helpful and valid outcomes.

Outcome Possibility 2

→ Adaptive teaching across the curriculum.
→ Adaptive teaching across the English curriculum.
→ Adaptive teaching across the secondary Spoken English curriculum.

→ How do teachers of secondary Spoken English adapt their teaching?

→ How do teachers of Spoken English adapt their Key Stage 3 teaching?

→ How do teachers of Spoken English adapt their Key Stage 3 teaching to accommodate children whose first language is not English?

→ How do teachers of Spoken English in a secondary school in Greater Manchester adapt their Key Stage 3 teaching to accommodate children whose first language is not English?

Outcome Possibility 3

→ Adaptive teaching across the curriculum.

→ Adaptive teaching across the English curriculum.

→ Adaptive teaching across the secondary English curriculum.

→ The use of assessment in adapting teaching across the secondary English curriculum.

→ The use of formative assessment in adapting teaching across the secondary English curriculum.

→ How do teachers of secondary English use formative assessment to adapt their teaching?

→ How do teachers of English in a secondary school in Greater Manchester use formative assessment to adapt their teaching?

Outcome Possibility 4

→ Adaptive teaching across the curriculum.

→ Adaptive teaching across the English curriculum.

→ Adaptive teaching across the secondary English curriculum.

→ The use of resources in adapting teaching across the secondary English curriculum.

→ Which resources do teachers of secondary English find most useful in adapting their teaching?

→ Which resources do teachers of secondary English find most useful in adapting their teaching, and why are these resources effective?

→ Which resources do teachers of secondary English find most useful in adapting their teaching, and why do they consider these resources to be effective?

→ Which resources do teachers of English in a secondary school in Greater Manchester find most useful in adapting their teaching, and why do they consider these resources to be effective?

It is possible that after interviewing or observing his participant teachers, Joshua's research question changes fundamentally. This is not common, but it has happened. For example, if in that last outcome possibility about exploring resources, it may transpire that participant teachers had little to say about resources but instead spent most of the time talking about routines, or streaming, or features of planning. If this was the case, then clearly resources were not the big thing amongst this particular group of participants. Joshua's title could rephrase to 'To what extent are resources important . . .' or change completely to 'Which aspects of classroom management do teachers of English . . .'.

Such a change of title is not an admission of defeat. On the contrary. It would show how Joshua had not confined his participants to rigidly exploring only those things that he had predetermined that he wanted them to talk about, but instead he had given them the headroom to tell him what they found to be more important in the field of adaptive practice. (See also Molly, Chapter 2). Joshua would be right to celebrate this change of title in his methodology so his marker can see how he allowed the voices of his participants to inform his focus. Of course, if the title changes significantly, aspects of the literature review may have to change accordingly too.

Activity 5.1

Consider one or more of these following fields. Adopting a similar process to the ones Joshua notionally went through with his supervisor, formulate a specific research question to suit the key stage and setting that you are teaching in or researching. As we saw from the possibilities in Joshua's consideration of his chosen field, there is no right or wrong outcome or destination for you here because the eventual outcome choice is informed by your setting, experience, and interests.

- Children's use of PE equipment.
- Children's career aspirations.
- Music teaching in the Early Years.
- Supporting children who have English as an Additional language.
- Early Career Teachers' experiences in their first year of teaching.
- Use of the interactive white board (or an innovative piece of software).
- Features of an effective behaviour management policy.
- Safeguarding children on the internet.
- Teachers' use of artificial intelligence.

DECIDING ON HOW TO EXPLORE YOUR QUESTION

Having established a workable research question (and remember that this may still evolve in the process of exploring it), it would be a strong thing to do in your research project to apply what has been covered in previous chapters. Let's return to Joshua. Joshua has chosen his field of adaptive teaching because he feels it is the weakest part of his professional practice, and he wants to expand his repertoire of strategies. For Joshua, the title he has decided to go with is "What factors inform differences in the ways teachers of English in a secondary school in Rochdale adapt their teaching for learners in Key Stages 3 and 4?" He will acknowledge within his introduction chapter that his is a problem of ignorance (ontology, Chapter 2), thus disclosing his positionality to his marker (Chapter 11), and giving context to his study. He wants examples and ideas to inform and improve his own practice, because the strategies he uses in Year 7 do not work well when he teaches Year 10 classes, and vice versa. Whilst acknowledging these things, he can also apply his research project to the Teachers' Standards (DfE, 2012) which his supervisor has told him would be a strong thing to do. Standard 5 reads 'Adapt teaching to respond to the strengths and needs of all pupils.'

All this context and preamble about problems of ignorance and professional development helps to inform Joshua's methodology. To gather his examples and ideas, he decides he would like to invite as many other teachers as possible who teach English across Key Stages 3 and 4 to let him observe them teaching (he is therefore conducting an instrumental case study, Chapter 3). He will tell the participants beforehand what his focus is (because of ethics – voluntary informed consent, Chapter 4). He will also interview each teacher individually if he can (Chapter 7). He still needs to decide whether he will observe each teacher first, and then interview them about what he has seen, or interview them first, and then watch them teach, armed with the information and insight they have given him in the interviews. He will make all these decisions clear in his methodology, together with his reasons for the order in which he chooses to do things.

If he sees interesting physical aspects of the classrooms (perhaps layout, environment, or resources) which seem relevant to adaptive teaching, or that the teachers tell him about, he will ask to photograph them before or after the children arrive or leave the rooms. This would further add to his triangulation and give additional context, as he would then be doing more than just interviewing and observing the teachers.

Joshua also fleetingly considers observing and interviewing a geography teacher whose teaching he admires, but he is worried that this will muddy the water and he would have to change his title (perhaps 'What factors inform differences in the ways teachers of English and Geography in a secondary school in Rochdale adapt their teaching for learners in Key Stages 3 and 4?'). But immediately, Joshua senses danger. Is he going to cling on to his agreed title or will he be flexible by accommodating the impressive geography teacher? Will such flexibility broaden and strengthen his study, or will it dilute his focus and cause problems? He does not know. Joshua is uncomfortably discovering that research needs discipline and consistent decision-making. He quickly decides not to interview the geography teacher after all. He wants to be faithful to his title. This is a methodological decision. His decision to be faithful to his title is now informing his method, and he will briefly refer to this decision in his methodology, even though it was a possible and plausible aspect of his method he consciously chose not to adopt.

All these decisions stem from the identification of a helpful research question: one that will enable Joshua to explore his interest in adaptive teaching with a number of teachers of English he respects. He is not trying to prove anything. He is not trying to show if or how adaptive teaching practices lead to better outcomes. He is collating information, taking a snapshot of the practices that apply within the school he is placed in. Nothing more.

RESEARCH QUESTIONS THAT SHOULD BE AVOIDED

There are few research questions or areas of focus that should, as a matter of policy, be outrightly avoided. Your supervisor may advise against, or even veto, sensitive areas such as sexuality, but amongst the students that we have supported over the years, the range of chosen areas of interest is extremely wide. You should try to go where your interest takes you.

It is very possible, however, that there could be a research interest that you, as an individual, should and must avoid. For example, Kate is doing a three-year Initial Teaching Training degree course, and in her first year, after an extremely successful teaching practice in a Reception class in an Essex primary school, she promised herself that she would become an Early Years practitioner once she completed her course. She kept in touch with the teachers at the setting, and they with her because they had been impressed with her teaching and professionalism. Her second-year placement was in a Year 2 classroom which she quite enjoyed, and her final year placement was in a Year 5 class which she disliked a lot because she found the pedagogy to be all very formal. During the final year of her course Kate was pleased when the school she had been in for her first-year placement invited her to apply for a position as a Year 1 teacher, to start the following September. Despite her promise to herself to find an Early Years position, she was very flattered to have been headhunted, and so she applied. After an interview which was harder than she imagined, they offered her the job. Kate still absolutely loved the school, so she accepted the position. However, immediately after accepting it she became worried whether she should have done so.

The problem for Kate was that she held strong (some might say narrow) views about creativity and play-based pedagogy and felt very comfortable in an Early Years environment in a way she had not in subsequent placements. She loved the playfulness of Early Years settings, and the way reception-aged children can learn through play and discovery. Her strongly held perception was that this Early Years pedagogy, which gives young children so much freedom and a good degree of autonomy, seemed to come to a crashing halt when children move to Year 1. Even though Kate loved the school where she had accepted the job, she did not want to be a teacher that delivered (in her mind) lesson after lesson of dry, planned whole-class activity, with imposed learning intentions and pre-determined assessment criteria.

To try to alleviate her concerns about accepting the job, Kate's intention for her research project was to explore and compare differences in the way children are taught either side of the transition from Reception to Year 1. She wants to explore teachers' perceptions of creativity on both sides of the divide, and to discover the extent to which she would be able (allowed?) to use play in her Year 1 classroom next year. She intends to interview Reception and Year 1 teachers in as many schools as she can, including her present placement school and the one she has been offered the job in. Kate tells all of this to her supervisor, expecting warm approval, as she has chosen an area of research that she is passionate about, and which will be relevant to her future professional practice.

--------- **Reflective Question 5.2** ---------

Please pause in your reading, and consider whether you can see any potential problems or conflicts of interest here? If you were Kate's supervisor, what advice would you give her?

There are four aspects of Kate's intended study and method which are ill-advised. The first is personal, the second methodological, the third surrounds definitions, and the fourth is ethical.

Firstly, even though the focus of her study is of itself perfectly valid and could make an interesting study in the hands of a different student, Kate is clearly incapable of taking a neutral dispassionate stance. Look at the vocabulary she has used with her supervisor – 'crashing halt', 'imposed learning intentions', 'allowed to use', 'across the divide'. It is all very sensationalist and defensive. Her supervisor considers that her binary and strongly held *'play-and-discovery-based-learning, good: whole-class-teaching-for-Year-1s, bad'* mentality is not going to allow her to take anything like an objective view. Primarily, Kate is not interested in identifying Year 1 teachers' perceptions of creativity and the transition between Reception and Year 1. Instead, her motivation comes from being a bit frightened about having accepted the job as a Year 1 teacher and hoping to find ways of protecting her class next year from what she perceives to be a required and overly formal Year 1 pedagogy. Kate's choice of focus is all about her own uncertain and scary situation, and that is a very poor rationale for choosing a research question. Her reading for her literature review is likely to be skewed and one-dimensional. She will seek out literature on the benefits of play and she will discount anything that speaks of the benefits of peer learning, social constructivism, and directed learning amongst Key Stage 1 children. Kate is unlikely to be able to recognise and include a compelling counterargument to her own views if she comes across one, because her mind is made up. Her choice of interview questions will be motivated by her own needs, and when analysing the data it is likely that Kate will give greater weight to those responses she empathises with, however much she will try not to. Her supervisor is of the view that, even though Kate is averaging high 60s for her assessed course submissions thus far, it would be unlikely she would be able to secure a good grade in her research project given the baggage she is bringing to it.

Secondly, from a methodological point of view, Kate intends to interview Reception teachers and Year 1 teachers, and talk to them about Year 1 pedagogy. It is highly likely that the Reception teachers will voice celebratory views about the benefits of Early Years pedagogies, yet Kate's research question is primarily about pedagogy in Year 1.

In interviewing Reception teachers, Kate is clinging to what she knows and is fishing for responses that mirror her own. If Kate is truly looking to explore play and creativity in Key Stage 1 and wants to include participant teachers from a relevant mix of Year groups, she would do better to interview Year 1 and 2 teachers, rather than Year 1 and Reception teachers.

Thirdly, Kate's definitions are ambiguous, and her supervisor thinks this is her biggest problem. She has made up her mind that play and creativity are the same thing, or at least are closely aligned, but she has yet to define either. Does play in a reception setting have to look the same as play in a Year 1 classroom? What is creativity and what does it look like in different contexts? Kate has yet to explore this satisfactorily with her supervisor because she has not yet considered these questions in her own mind. This is the source of her anxiety about the Year 1 job, and it would be very unwise for her to decide to unpick these questions in an assessed research project so that she is in a better position to grapple with her own professional anxieties. A research project is not a good arena for the exploration of personal difficulties (professional interests or professional development, yes: personal difficulties, no).

Fourthly, the ethics of involving teachers in the school that Kate has been offered a job in will not be allowed by her supervisor, and rightly so. She has an obvious vested interest in that school, and involving those teachers, essentially to inform her own career choices, would constitute a clear conflict of interest.

Kate's situation demonstrates that there are research questions that must be avoided because research is a two-way street. In our experience, the criterion for deciding not to embark on a contentious research focus is more likely to be found in you, the researcher, than in the question itself.

You may be interested to know that Kate did not withdraw from the Year 1 job, and only a few days after starting her job realised that despite her initial reservations, there were any number of opportunities for the incorporation of creative professional practice and play in Year 1. She worked very happily in the school, and still does. Her definition of what constitutes 'play' broadened enormously during her Early Career Teacher years. Her final choice of research project title was 'What recognised theoretical positions concerning learning and teaching are contained in the national curriculum (2013), either overtly or implied, and how are they outworked in Key Stage 1 classrooms in a primary school in Essex?'. Both she and her supervisor agreed it was rather a long title, but all attempts to shorten it led to frustration. Her submission attracted a grade of 78%.

SUMMARY

The main points we hope you will have taken from this chapter are:

- Your choice of focus is yours to make based upon your interests and/or professional development.
- A research question is more helpful than a research statement.
- Make your research question specific in terms of setting, age, and focus.
- Your research question, if it is a strong one, will inform your research methods but it will not dictate the outcomes.

- We do not recommend choosing a research project focus that you hope will inform a professional decision you need to make, or that explores something you are angry about.

======= Activity 5.2 =======

1 Consider what motivated you to choose your research question or focus. Why do you think it is an important or useful question, and who is it important or useful to? It will strengthen your research project if you know the significance or purpose of your question, and this will help you to remain motivated through the research process as well, even if things get messy or overwhelming (which often happens in research).

2 What have you learnt about creating a research question?

3 You may want to share your research question with someone who can give you insights, ideas and advice or to support you further, for example a research supervisor, a teacher or headteacher, or a fellow student. Do not feel that all the ideas for your project have to come from you.

FURTHER READING

Burton, N, Brundrett, M. and Jones, M. (2014). *Doing your education research project*. 2nd edn. London: SAGE.

If you are a trainee teacher or experienced practitioner new to research, or are simply wondering how to get started on your education research project, this practical book will be your guide. The authors offer simple steps to ensure that you ask the key questions in the most effective way possible. The book guides you through the entire research process: from clarifying the context and conceptual background, to presenting and analysing the evidence gathered.

Creswell, J.W. and Creswell, J.D. (2022). *Research design: Qualitative, quantitative, and mixed methods approaches*. 6th edn. Thousand Oaks, CA: SAGE.

This sixth edition provides clear and concise instruction for designing research projects or developing research proposals. This user-friendly text walks readers through research methods, from reviewing the literature to writing a research question and stating a hypothesis to designing the study.

DfE. (2011, terminology updated 2021). *Teachers' standards guidance for school leaders, school staff and governing bodies*. Crown copyright.

These standards set the minimum requirements for teachers' practice and conduct.

Punch, K. and Oancea, A. (2014). *Introduction to research methods in education*. 2nd edn. London: SAGE.

This book introduces the research process in a range of educational contexts. In this updated second edition, you'll find guidance on every stage of research, with chapters on developing research questions, doing a literature review, collecting data, analysing your findings and writing it all up.

6

RESEARCH WITH CHILDREN

================= **Chapter Aims** =================

- An identification of different methods and strategies for involving children in research.
- Collecting data with very young children (0–5).

WHY UNIVERSITIES OFTEN DISCOURAGE STUDENTS FROM UNDERTAKING RESEARCH INVOLVING CHILDREN

The most compelling aspect of undertaking research involving children must be ethics. Chapter 4 explores key aspects of ethics, in which we demonstrate how detailed you must be in an ethics application, but producing an ethics proposal to secure ethical approval is one thing, whereas conducting an ethical piece of research from conception to conclusion is quite another. In research, unexpected situations arise. For students, these usually arise in either the recruitment stage, or in the data collection stage. For example, children (of whatever age) may be uncooperative, despite having agreed to take part, or they may say unexpected or unguarded things. Similarly, student researchers might be tempted (consciously or unconsciously) to take short cuts, or to put themselves in vulnerable safeguarding situations. It might be tempting for data to be manipulated or omitted to make children's responses support the research question more compellingly. Coupled with this, the only control a university has over the course of a research project occurs during the ethics application stage, and via the supervisor, who is not present during the recruitment and data collection period, when unexpected things can start to happen. Your university is therefore reliant on students being faithful to what they say will happen in their proposals, but since it is likely that you, a reader of this book, will have prior experience of the organic environments which are schools, you will appreciate that what is planned and what subsequently happens can be very different things. For this reason, universities often discourage or even forbid students from involving children directly in research projects.

But this is a book about doing research in schools, so if you are minded to involve children in your research (anyone under the age of 18), and your university or

institution is happy to allow you to do so, this chapter will give you help and suggestions as to how you might do it. The chapter explores the following:

- interviewing children;
- observing children;
- using children's existing work;
- giving children tasks to do;
- tracking children;
- research with children under five.

INTERVIEWING CHILDREN

We offer here some tried and tested strategies that will enhance your interviews with
children.

Strategy 1: Acknowledge to Yourself and to the Children That the Child Is the Expert

As adults we have forgotten what it is to think and speak like a child. Five-year-old
children are not experts in many things, but they are experts in being five. Certainly,
they are more expert in that than you are. So if, for example, you want to discover five-
years-olds' experiences and perceptions of developing throwing and catching ball skills,
you have to speak in the language of a five-year-old; you must ask questions that will
encourage and allow a five-year-old to want to speak about it; and, most importantly,
throughout the interview, you must listen without converting or translating what is said
into adult-speak. You want children to feel that they are the experts. For example, if
twelve-year-olds tell you about their experiences of the transition from primary to
secondary school, tell them that you know nothing about it, because things have
changed since it happened to you. By acknowledging this to them, you empower them.
If they know that they are educating you, telling you things about an experience they
have had of which you have no experience or pre-conception, they will want to help
you, and they will expand on what they say to help you understand. The same is true of
fourteen-year-olds who are telling you about their career aspirations. An important
strategy in interviewing children is to make them feel valuable. Shift the power dynamic
as much as you can. They are the experts; make sure they know this.

Strategy 2: Do Not Interrupt

A second strategy in successfully interviewing children is to avoid interrupting them.
Give them time to complete what they have to say. Do not finish their sentences. This
can be particularly hard with children under the age of about seven, who often must
take two or three run ups to a sentence to finally complete it, because at the start of it
they have not yet formulated in their minds the vocabulary they want to use to get to
the end, and so on each attempt they get a bit further each time. You can see the end of
the sentence before they can. But still, do not interrupt. Yes, you can repeat and clarify

what they are saying during the interview if that is appropriate, but in doing so, do not couch their responses in adult vocabulary. If, when summarising or confirming their responses, you happen to misconstrue or subtly change the meaning of what eight-year-olds are saying, they will not correct you. The power dynamics are such that this will not happen. The same is likely to be true of a secondary school child, unless they are very confident. You must listen, even if you think you know where their responses are going, and even if it is taking them an age to say it.

It is easy to clumsily get in the way of children's responses, or to accidently shut down a promising line of conversation by trying to confirm or to summarise it. To avoid this, a successful strategy we have used is to ask children to clarify or repeat, rather than doing this yourself. You might adopt phrases like 'I'm really interested in that. Can you tell me more?', or 'I want to make sure I really understand what you are saying. Can you tell me that again, please?'. This avoids the need for the interviewer to summarise what children have said using words even an adult would understand.

Strategy 3: Do Not Anticipate the Answers You Want in the Delivery of the Questions, or by Over-Guiding

Wouldn't it be awful if, when listening to recordings of interviews with children, you discovered that the person who said the most was you. This is a very common feature of inexperienced researchers' interview transcripts of children. You become so busy directing the children, asking questions which you then rephrase and amplify to make sure they understand, that you forget to give them time and space to think for themselves. This is because you do not trust them to understand your subtext or to faithfully follow your expected line of enquiry.

Kayley is interviewing a group of Year 5 children about the extent to which they use the displays in the classroom to help them with their writing. There are five children in the group, two boys and three girls. The interview is taking place in their classroom.

Kayley: *This is lovely bright classroom. I love all the displays. They look really helpful. There's some about maths, and a science one. For this interview I am interested in the ones over here that help you with your writing. Do you use them much? I see there's a spelling word bank, and VCOP one. I'm interested to know how much you use them, or what you use them for.* [very short pause] *For example, do you like to use the word bank, or do you prefer to think of your own words? Did you suggest any of the words on the word bank? Or the list of punctuation. Does that help you to use different punctuation marks or perhaps, you know, maybe that makes you feel pressured into using punctuation that you otherwise might not? So I'm interested to know how you use the displays when you are writing.* [pause] *Who'd like to start?* [pause] *Chris?*

Chris: Erm, ...

Meanwhile, in a different school, but also with Year 5, Harriet has the same idea for her research project. Here is part of the transcript from her interview.

Harriet:	*This is lovely bright classroom. I love all the displays. These ones look really good. Would you mind telling me about them?* [pause, in truth slightly longer than Harriet was comfortable with]
Chris:	Miss Collins puts words up there we can use . . .
Jessica:	(interrupting) . . .Yeah, it helps spelling.
John:	I don't use it much. I did once, cos Miss Collins said I should, but I don't.
Francesca:	Two of those words are mine. Pigeon and Trafalgar. They're hard to sp. . .
Harriet:	*Pigeon and Trafalgar?*
Francesca:	There was a picture.
Harriet:	*Ah. Do you use it, Jessica?*
Jessica:	Sometimes, but it slows me down. I forget what I want to write sometimes . . .
Chris:	That happens to me too. I try and write something, and if I look up and I don't write it quickly, I forget . . .
John:	(interrupting) I'm a good writer. I don't need it.

Harriet is discovering all sorts of things that are relevant to her research question (which focuses on the efficacy of displays in children's writing), but the responses are not only about the children's use of the displays to help their writing. She is also learning about Year 5 children's experiences of the process of writing that she was not expecting to hear about. She will have a great deal of data to sift through. Her research question may change somewhat as a result, but that is a good thing because this shows she has not predestined what the responses of her participants might be by telling them what to say. Kayley, by contrast, gave her Year 5s no wriggle room at all. Her data is likely to be very thin and will have no surprises.

So, when interviewing children, do not overwhelm them with questions which have multiple components. You risk ending up with a transcript that is mainly you talking as you painstakingly direct the conversation to your own purposes. Yes, be aware of the intended direction of travel. Have a loose plan (a semi-structured interview would be a recommendation) but do not impose yourself on the interview.

▬▬▬▬ Activity 6.1 ▬▬▬▬

Spend some time listening to the way good radio presenters interview politicians or celebrities. Note how the presenters often ask questions with multiple components, and in so doing they effectively answer their own question, inviting (or expecting) the interviewee to agree, and often leaving very little time between each question before interrupting. They do this because they are trying to control what is said. You should try not to do that. Yes, there is safety in control, but a strong and confident student researcher will relinquish tight control of interviews in exchange for a greater opportunity to hear children's or adult participants' own voice. If you are hearing surprises, that means you are allowing your participants to articulate their own views, and not just to confirm yours.

OBSERVING CHILDREN

Observing children or adults is a very common aspect of social science research. It sounds straightforward, but it comes with difficulties. You may have heard of two real obstacles to collecting authentic social research data, namely Social Desirability Bias, and the Hawthorne effect. The first relates to ways in which people seek to please or conform, individually or as a group. This can be a real problem if you collect data from children whom you know. Perhaps you have been teaching the children during your school placement and so they feel they know you and want to help you. The second speaks of the way people change their behaviour when they know they are being watched, not necessary to please or to conform, but simply because they are being observed. They may therefore amplify, exaggerate or artificially minimise their movements and behaviours. Children may engage with resources that they otherwise would not be interested in, or vice versa, simply because they know they are being watched. It is a particular problem in social science research, because you are required to tell participants what the focus of your research is, but this can inevitably influence what participants say in interviews, or what they do when being observed.

We identify here strategies you may choose to adopt when observing children. Some will mitigate for Social Desirability Bias and the Hawthorne effect. Some may not. But you are advised to acknowledge these two impediments to authentic data collection in the methodology chapter of your research project, and it will help you to take them into account when observing children.

Strategy 1. Are You an Active or a Passive Observer?

Decide whether you are going to be an active participant in what is being observed, or a passive distant observer. Either choice will appear rather unusual to the children. Will you be with the children, actively driving an activity, perhaps explaining a task, drawing with them, or accompanying them? This does not in itself jeopardise the validity of your research, but you should be aware that the children will find it a bit odd if you are simultaneously making notes about what they say and do or perhaps audio recording their conversations if you have never done this whilst being with them before. Or will you instead be a remote fly on the wall, sitting unobtrusively away from what is going on, making no contribution to what is being observed beyond the possible setting-up of the activity or environment in the first place? If you have spent the last ten weeks in your school placement sitting with the children, teaching them, engaging with them, being interested in them, it would surely serve to exacerbate the Hawthorne effect if you were to then suddenly separate yourself from them during an activity. They would rightly wonder why your behaviour had changed so radically. 'Ah', they would notionally think to themselves, 'this is clearly the observation she spoke about last week. We must all behave normally' and they would then go out of their way to behave 'normally'.

Most student teachers undertaking a research project initially think that observation must be a distant thing and consider that if the children were to notice them making observations, this would diminish the value of the observation. This is not true. Observation need not be a furtive thing. You do not have to be in disguise, camouflaged, unattainable, or hidden. You can be in the thick of it. But you do need to decide which approach you will adopt. Neither is wrong. The setting can make a difference to your choice, of course. Observing differences in how reception children engage in an outdoor environment on a rainy day as opposed to a dry one is a very different exercise to observing how Year 9 children make use of dictionaries.

Strategy 2. Make Many Observations

It is likely that you as a trainee teacher will undertake your research project in the school in which you do your final teaching placement. It is also likely that you will know that this will be the case weeks ahead of your data collection period. It is therefore a good idea for you to adopt some of the behaviours that you will use for your project in the weeks leading up to it. For example, if you were to regularly sit with the children and make notes about what they are doing, perhaps making your assessments as you go along, they will be intrigued at first, and then after a while they will consider it normal behaviour on your part. This is good assessment practice anyway, because you can talk to the children as you are assessing them, involving them meaningfully in the process, and it will also save you time in the long run, but such professional practice lies outside of your research project. As such, you will still need to tell the children your purposes when the data collection for your project begins, but your normalised behaviour will remain and will not be a distraction. (This is because you must remember the distinction between your identity as a trainee teacher and that as a researcher, even though you are working with the same children.) This is likely to at least reduce Social Desirability Bias or the Hawthorne effect (but will not completely remove them). Similarly, if you know you are going to place a microphone or audio recording device on a table to capture conversations while the children undertake an activity that you intend to observe during your research project, design a different activity or two whereby this happens during lessons in the weeks preceding your data collection. You would need a reason for doing this – it would look very odd if you just recorded their conversations for no discernible reason. Perhaps you will play the recordings back to them in groups and ask the children to give their reaction to it in terms of their learning or engagement.

But the microphone or audio recording device would not become a sudden imposition initiated at the onset of your research project. It would be, if not normal, at least familiar.

USING CHILDREN'S WORK

Be very clear in your own mind why you want to do this. Remember the children must not be identifiable. All primary school teachers and many secondary school teachers can identify children's work from the handwriting and other features of the work, just as you can often know the sender of a birthday card just from looking at the envelope.

As with instrumental or intrinsic case studies (Chapter 3) it is important to be clear what you are trying to achieve. Are you looking at the work of children across a year group? Perhaps you are investigating what commonalities appear in the writing of Year 3 children or those in Year 11; or you are exploring common mathematical misconceptions amongst Year 9s; or the typical amount of work produced in different timescales in Year 4. By contrast, it may be that you are interested in how punctuation use develops across Key Stage 2, so you are counting and contextualising exclamation marks, full stops, speech marks and capital letters. In all these cases you are seeking to involve as many children as is manageable. As with our advice about intrinsic case studies in Chapter 3, you should not explore a single child's work, or that of a small selection of children. The risk of harm or of identifiability is too great.

If you intend to take any of these approaches, it would be ethically much safer to ask children to generate writing (or mathematical calculations, or any other 'product' of relevance to your research question) specifically for your project, so that you could analyse it across the cohort.

Using Children's Existing Work

Be very careful about using children's existing work. Grace is on her final placement in a Year 4 class. She has had a bit of luck, and a good idea (she thinks). A Year 2 teacher has told her about a dusty box in a cupboard containing English workbooks from two years ago, which were collected for an Ofsted inspection, and then set aside for reasons no one can remember. Grace decides she will compare these Year 2 workbooks with the current Year 4 English workbooks (who are, therefore, the same children) firstly as a cohort, and then for triangulation she will show the books to the children and get them to identify and talk about ways in which their own writing has changed.

━━━━━━━ Reflective Questions 6.1 ━━━━━━━

Please stop reading for a moment, to think whether you see any significant ethical problems or sensitivities here? There are always ethical sensitivities, and this example contains a big one. Can you see it already, before we point out.

Two ethical aspects arise here. Firstly, (as with Saira's intended use of children's End of Key Stage 3 and Key Stage 4 progress data: in Chapter 4) Grace is intending to help herself to children's work from two years ago for purposes that it was not originally intended for. She is, therefore, not entitled to it without the written permission of parents and children (permission which Grace thinks is likely to be forthcoming, because surely, she thinks, everyone would be interested – but Grace would be surprised to be wrong). Secondly, there is a much more significant and sensitive aspect. Here is the potential and quite likely scenario. On seeing the work by his younger self, Year 4 Toby is really pleased to see how his writing has developed from when he was in Year 2, and how his handwriting has improved. Celia is similarly excited and proud. By contrast,

Nathan, who struggles with his writing at the best of times, cannot see much change, even though he really tries at it, and has done so consistently for the last two years. His spelling is still as erratic as it was, and if anything, his handwriting has got bigger and messier. His heart sinks. Why bother? In her enthusiasm for what she was certain was a great idea for a research project, Grace has hurt Nathan more than she could imagine or know. Furthermore, for safeguarding reasons, having read the advice in this book (Chapter 5), Grace would have chosen to meet the children in groups (not individually) to share the workbooks with them. Nathan would therefore endure this deeply negative and traumatic experience in the full glare of some of his excited classmates. He will be years recovering, if he recovers at all.

We are not saying that Grace should not undertake any aspect of this research if she can secure permissions, but she needs to ensure that nobody is going to get hurt. If she can get enough permission slips returned, she might compare the books across some of the cohort, but even this is dangerous, as she would be raising interest in the Year 2 books. As we have seen from her emotional assault of Nathan, she would be ill-advised to ask the children to identify their own progress. If even one person is likely to be harmed, it cannot happen for anybody. Grace needs to have the protection of Nathan's self-esteem front and centre, and she needs to put her own aspirations firmly at the bottom of the pile.

GIVING CHILDREN TASKS TO DO

This is a common method, popular with both students and children, because children need not be self-conscious about what they say or how their views might be interpreted, and it can generate very unexpected data. Here are five examples of how giving tasks for children to do has enhanced students' research projects. A sixth example can be found below under 'Successful tasks, activities and strategies with under-fives', but which can be adapted to be applicable to older children and even adults too.

Example 1

For her research project, Sumaiya, a trainee science teacher in a secondary school in Norwich, wants to explore children's gender perceptions of different career options. Rather than just asking children about their perceptions, Sumaiya wants to identify subconscious attitudes and biases, so she intends to ask children in Year 8 and Year 10 to each draw a picture of a scientist and a pilot at work. Predominantly she is anticipating pictures of males, but she hopes to be wrong. Sumaiya will then ask the children to give the people they have drawn a name; ask them why they have chosen to draw the pictures as they have; and how they might have drawn the picture differently. Note that Sumaiya has not asked why they have drawn a picture of a female or male but instead has only asked gender-neutral questions which do not lead the children in a particular direction. Sumaiya then asks the children to draw another person of the same career. This gives the children the opportunity to double down on their gender perception, or not, and to incorporate details they might have omitted earlier, or want to include having had the discussion and heard other children's ideas. Sumaiya has decided to analyse the pictures and responses under three phases. Firstly, an analysis of the first picture each child drew; secondly, the discussions; and thirdly, the second picture. There is a lot going on here for Sumaiya. She needs to know which picture is which and who has said what about which pictures, and she wants to analyse the data both as separate Year 8 and Year 10 cohorts, and to separate the data of male and female participants. It is high concentration on Sumaiya's part, but she thinks it will be worth it. To make it manageable, she has decided to undertake the tasks in small groups of three or four children each time. Finally, in a fourth consecutive phase, Sumaiya talks to the children directly about the reasons behind the tasks they have just done, and their perceptions of girls in Science, Technology, Engineering and Mathematics (STEM) careers, or boys in caring professions, which would have been her starting point had she not had the drawing task idea, and she will go on to ask them how these perceptions resonated (or not) with the pictures the children have just drawn.

This career gender approach is not a research question exclusive to secondary schools. We have supervised similar projects in Key stage 2 and even Key Stage 1 (under the title of 'People Who Help Us' and without the use of the word 'career'). In different contexts you might, for example, ask children to draw a vet, or a doctor, a computer programmer, a teacher, a politician, a stay-at-home parent, an engineer, a nurse, a dancer, a sports person, a shop worker, or an electrician.

Example 2

Edward is interested in Year 6 children's strategies for doing mental arithmetic calculations in multiplication and division, and particularly their use of counting on fingers. His interest was sparked on hearing a chance remark from one child saying to others (rather proudly) that she no longer needed to count on her fingers, and he noted that the other children looked either quizzical or impressed. Edward still counts on his fingers, always has, and it has never occurred to him not to. Before interviewing children about their mental arithmetic strategies, Edward decides to sit with groups of children whilst they do mental arithmetic tasks, during which he will observe and note (without the use of photography, of course) their physical strategies (eye movement, rhythmic nodding, miming or counting out loud, use of fingers). In this way he generates a good deal of data even before the children have said anything about their preferences or attitudes. Edward will go on to ask them about their strategies generally, and then about their attitudes to counting on their fingers. Only after the children's attitudes have been revealed, Edward intends to tell them that he has always counted on his fingers and to ask them whether they think this is odd behaviour in an adult. He will do this because he does not want any of the children feeling babyish or ashamed of their use of counting on fingers. He also has a YouTube video to show them of people (adults and children) across the world using their hands in very different ways when doing arithmetical tasks. Edward is not trying to change perceptions. He is merely interested to find whether these Year 6 children think counting on fingers is perhaps a phase they will grow out of, or essential to an understanding of our number system, or something else.

Example 3

Jane has noted how after her Year 3 children have done a piece of writing, the class teacher often asks them to draw a picture, depicting what they have written about. Jane, who has a keen interest in art, wonders what would happen if the children did the drawing before the writing, in order that the children might be able to visually plan or at least pre-empt what they were likely to write about. Jane is not intending to do pre- and post-comparisons of what children produce, as she does not want to base her research project on only two pieces of writing per child, and, more importantly, she does not want to upset her host teacher by giving the impression that she (Jane) thinks the teacher is doing things the wrong way round. Instead, Jane intends to read the children a story, ask them to choose one part of it to draw, then get them to write that part of the story that they have drawn, and finally to interview them about how they found the experience regarding their enjoyment and/or success in doing the writing.

Example 4

Arthur is exploring Key Stage 2 boys' reading preferences, so he asks participants to select three books from a selection of eighteen contrasting titles and genres. Three of the books he provides are picture story books; three are children's novels. Three are poetry books; three are non-fiction. Three are audio books. Arthur has also covered three books of contrasting size and weight in plain brown paper, which the children are allowed to choose should they want to, but they are not allowed to touch these covered books before they make their selection. Note that Arthur has given three of each type of book so that if any of the children want to take all three of their picks from the same genre, they can, but they don't have to. Arthur will ask the children about their choices later, and he will also ask them if they would like to read one of the books to or with him, or whether they would prefer to read it alone (he is not sure whether or not this question will generate interesting data, but he is including it just in case). During the boys' selection process, Arthur will note the extent to which the children start to read some of the book before making their choice, or whether they just flick through some of the pages (or whether they don't do any of that).

In doing all this, Arthur is giving the children a helpful starting point for the interviews that he will conduct later that day, a starting point which is already centred on the child, enabling him to ease them into the interview. The questions 'I noticed you three boys took all your choices from the non-fiction options. Tell me what you like about non-fiction', or 'I noticed all four of you took three very different types of books. That's really interesting. Tell me why you chose those' are much better starting points than 'What sort of books do you most like reading?', which would have been a very dry early interview question had Arthur not engaged the children in the choosing activity. Also, Arthur was surprised to realise that on those occasions when he was able to interview children who had made similar choices, they often talked freely about their preferences to each other, safe in the knowledge that they were amongst like-minded children. In some of these interviews, Arthur hardly had to say much at all, just steering the conversations from time to time when necessary. He had not planned that and found it very pleasing. He also reported it in the conclusion of his submitted research project as a successful methodological feature.

You may be interested to know that the question about whether the children would prefer to read with Arthur or without generated a broad range of responses, and without an age pattern. Arthur had assumed that the younger children (Year 3 and 4) would mainly want to read to or with him, and the older children would not, but the responses fell about half and half across all four of the year groups. This was an unexpected finding that Arthur was able to report in his data analysis. By contrast, of Arthur's 15 participants, only one boy chose one of the plain covered books, and when asked about it, could not say why. Arthur wished he had not bothered with that idea, not least because it took him a long time to put the covers on the books. Sometimes research ideas work. Sometimes they just don't.

Example 5

Bethan's teaching placement is in a secondary school, and she has offered to help with library supervision at lunchtime once a week. Beyond the low-level occasional behaviour management problems, she is surprised how much help the younger children seem to need to find things, so her intended research project title is 'What support or training do Key Stage 3 children in a secondary school in South East Wales feel they would most benefit from to help them become autonomous users of their school library?'. Bethan could have explored this question by simply observing participating children's use of the library, and then interviewing them about their needs, but instead she asked the school for permission to close the library for three consecutive lunchtimes so she could give groups of children limited time to undertake specific tasks. First, they were asked to discuss how they might do the tasks, and then they were asked to fulfil them. Tasks included finding things such a specific book, or the details of a historical event, or of a scientific phenomenon. Another task was to give the children a problem to solve, such as planning and costing a trip. A third task was to reorder books on a shelf which had become rather disorganised, and to reshelve a returned book.

Again, as with Arthur and Sumaiya above, the tasks enabled Bethan to begin her subsequent interviews from a position of informed strength. The question 'How did you get on with finding information about the differences between viruses and bacteria?' is much better than 'How do you go about finding information in the library'?

Bethan experienced what she mistakenly thought was a tricky ethical dilemma after her research. The school was keen to improve the efficacy of the library, and to this end, Mrs Goddard, a deputy head, was interested know Bethan's findings and asked if she could see them. Bethan politely explained that she could share her finished research project with the school, but the data itself, the children's responses and her observation notes of specific children undertaking the tasks, were protected for confidentiality by her ethics commitments. In fact, Bethan had misunderstood what the deputy head had asked for. Deputy heads tend to know a lot about data protection and Mrs Goddard knew not to ask for Bethan's original data. She was asking only for the overall findings. Nonetheless, Mrs Goddard was pleased that Bethan had chosen to be a faithful guardian of her data, knowing that it takes a lot of confidence to deny a request from a deputy head.

TRACKING CHILDREN

If you were to undertake a literature search for published research which focuses on tracking school children, most results, by a large proportion, would be articles surrounding academic progress. We do not recommend that you track children's academic progress for your research project. For one thing, tracking tends to be a longitudinal activity, and you are unlikely to have the time to identify changes in children's progress in the amount of time you have at your disposal to undertake your project. Secondly, the academic tracking of children tends to be because of interest in assessing the impact of an intervention or change, and unless the variables can be minimised, it is hard to identify cause and effect. Such a piece of action research is beyond the intended scope of an assessed research project.

If you were to take a broader definition of 'tracking', however, you might want to track behaviours or experiences. For example, if you were interested in discovering what the experiences of Year 8 children are during a typical day at school, you might shadow a class, which could generate or inform all sorts of interesting research questions. What variety of tasks are they asked to do in a day? How much autonomy or agency do they have over what they are asked to do, or how they might do it? How much of what they experience in a typical day is new learning, how much is consolidation, how much is mastery? How much is kinaesthetic? What different strategies are used by teachers to welcome children at the start of lessons and to get them engaged? What are the energy levels at different times of day? Such studies would contribute to your professional development and might enable you to become a more empathetic teacher, particularly perhaps in the afternoons or just before lunch.

You might also track children's use of space or equipment in breaktimes or lessons, such as music (which instruments or resources are most popular?). Which parts of the library are most/least used? What activities are most common in the staffroom?

RESEARCH WITH CHILDREN UNDER FIVE

There are two tricky aspects to this. The first, of course, is ethics (in particular, informed consent and securing permissions) and the second is logistics (methods and collecting useful data). The people responsible for giving you ethical approval within your university or institution will increase their scrutiny of all aspects of your proposal when they see you are involving very young children, and rightly so.

Regarding securing permissions, you must remember that the BERA guidelines (2024) require all participants to opt in, so it is not enough to simply ask the parents to opt in on behalf of their children. The children must be told what is going to happen. You must be convinced that they understand what will happen, and that they genuinely want to take part. To this end, your research method must be primarily designed to interest them. They must enjoy the tasks or experiences if they are to engage in them for a useful amount of time. This is not to say that they need to know what an assessed research project is, but they do need to know what they will be asked to do; to know that they can stop doing it any time they like (which is already very common day-to-day practice in Early Years settings); and to know that you would like to make notes about it. They do not need to know about data protection (but the parents do, of course).

You will also need to demonstrate to your marker and to the ethics committee how the children will opt in. Below is an example of a child-friendly permission slip. It would be advisable to read the information to younger children and they can indicate their consent by pointing to or colouring in an 'emoji-type' icon to express their preference. This can be adapted for older children, for example, in key stage two by using more age-appropriate language and then writing their preference as well as their name and the inclusion of a signature.

■■■■■■ Child-Friendly Permission Slip ■■■■■■

[This bit can be read out]

Who Is This Information Sheet For?
This information sheet is for you children in this school/my class to take part in a writing project!

I would like you (*insert child's name here*) to help me with 'Put the title of your research project here'.

It is important for you to understand why my writing project is being done and what you will have to do. Please listen as I read the following information carefully. You can choose if you want to help me!

What Is the Purpose of the Writing Project?
The project aims to explore...................... (put the brief information from the research project proposal here).

Why Am I Choosing You?
I am a trainee teacher within your school, and I need your help in getting some information from you. This will help me to become a better teacher. You can help me if you want to with my project because you know about how things work in this school. What you say, do or write can help me.

What Will You Be Asked to Do?
I shall be asking you to............. (talk in an interview, or write in a questionnaire, or let me watch you learn. State intended time frame, length of interview or brief outline of data collection).

(Continued)

(Continued)

I promise that I will keep all my notes very safe and not let anyone see them. No-one else, apart from my helper and me, will know what you said or did.

Please know that:

- You can stop helping me at any time you choose.
- You don't need to answer questions or write anything that you don't want to.
- No-one will know what you said, wrote or did from my writing.

Your Bit:

- I have listened to my trainee teacher tell me all about the writing.
- I want to take part in this project (Figure 6.1).

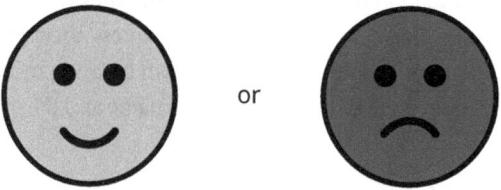

Figure 6.1 Happy and Sad Faces Used to Indicate a Child's Willingness to Participate

Write the name of child here:
Date:
This project is externally supervised by:
Researcher's main supervisor's contact details:

Regarding logistics, very young children are extremely trusting, and very sensitive to changes in environments and routines. As a result, your research project will not be successful if you simply impose yourself and your methodology on an unsuspecting four-year-old. If you are insensitive to the norms of the setting, the children will not engage with you. Neither will the school allow you to do that. For example, if you try to sit very young children down and interview them, this is unlikely to be successful because nobody has done that with them before and they will be suddenly apprehensive and wary. But if you sit with them while they are playing or doing activities and ask them what they are doing and why, they will be only too pleased to tell you all sorts of things, much of which will be relevant to your study (and much will not). You can also observe how they are going about their task; the social nature of it perhaps, or the problem-solving strategies. If children veer off in their talking to things which are irrelevant to your study, do not try to bring them back immediately. You must wait. If you are lucky, they will return. Yes, you can repeat or rephrase your question a little later, but if you are truly interested in the voice of the child, no amount of prompting will help your study if very young children are not interested in what you are talking to them about.

SUCCESSFUL TASKS, ACTIVITIES AND STRATEGIES WITH UNDER-FIVES

Tasks and activities you might ask children to do, or strategies you might use, that have proved successful in research projects we have supervised are as follows.

Role Play With Dolls or Puppets

Children will often talk to a puppet or doll rather more openly than to an adult. Perhaps Sukie the rag doll has difficulty remembering what expectations of behaviour are in different parts of the classroom, or which toys can only be used in the sand pit and which toys should never be in there. Perhaps Dylan the puppet has never played in the outdoor area and wants to know from the children what they like to do most out there.

Ask the Children to Show You Round the Classroom or Other Environment

A tour of a classroom or outdoor area with young children will not be like a tour of a house from an estate agent, but were you to ask children to show you things in the classroom and tell you about them, they will show you the places they like best, or the things they most like doing, or the things that are most important to them. This will identify to you some of their values and preferences in their learning. For example, Harini undertook an insightful research project using this method and discovered that hardly any of the children drew her attention to anything above their own eye level. Several children showed Harini where craft materials were kept. Several showed her the book area. None showed her the carpet area where they sat for directed learning or any of the displays. Harini later asked the children in passing (during a sorting activity) what the carpet was for, and they told her, generally with some enthusiasm, that this was where they sat with the teacher. It was clear from the way they spoke that they liked being on the carpet area, but it was interesting that no child thought to show it to her, as they had the scissors drawer or the water tray. There was a lot for Harini to unpick, and all from asking the children to share their perceptions of their learning space, instead of asking them direct questions. Imagine if Harini's research question had been specifically about the book corner, or children's safe use of tools. She would have focused only on that question, and collected data about that specific thing, perhaps watching them gluing, bolting, spooning, measuring and hammering things and asking them about what they were doing. This would have been a safe, valid, predetermined research focus, which despite its premeditated nature had the potential for a strong grade from her marker. But instead, Harini allowed her final research question (*'What aspects of an Early Years classroom in a primary school in Northwest Kent are most prominent in the perceptions of reception-aged children?'*) to be informed by the preferences and experiences of the children. She did not impose a pre-selected question on the children or choose a classroom area of interest on their behalf, and in doing so Harini discovered all sorts of things about children's interaction and relationship with their learning environment, which in turn informed her future professional practice.

SUMMARY

The main messages we hope you take from this chapter are:

- We have given examples of a selection of strategies, methods and techniques that have been used with various resulting degree of success by students under our supervision to collect data from children, some of which you may choose to emulate, and some we hope you will choose not to.

FURTHER READING

British Educational Research Association (BERA). (2024). *Ethical guidelines for educational research*, 5th edn. [Online] Available at: https://www.bera.ac.uk/publication/ethical-guidelines-for-educational-research-fifth-edition-2024-online (accessed: January 2025).

The intended audience for these guidelines is anyone undertaking educational research – whether their job description includes research, or they conduct research within the field (for example, while studying for a qualification or with the intention of improving practice). This includes both independent researchers and practitioners based in educational institutions of any kind.

Johnson, V., Hart, R., & Colwell, J. (2014). *Steps to engaging young children in research.* University of Brighton. Bernard van Lear Foundation.

This guide has been developed to support researchers to include young children in research; particularly children aged 5–8 years of age. While it has been designed to support those who are seeking to include young children in research for the first time it is hoped that the broad range of methods described will also be of value for more seasoned researchers.

O' Leary, Z. (2014). 'Undertaking credible and ethical research', in O' Leary, Z. *Doing your research project.* London: SAGE, pp. 47–71.

This chapter is essential in reminding researchers of their research obligations: legal, moral, and ethical.

Ponizovsky-Bergelson, Y., Dayan, Y., Wahle, N., & Roer-Strier, D. (2019). 'A qualitative interview with young children: what encourages or inhibits young children's participation?' *International Journal of Qualitative Methods*, *18*. https://doi.org/10.1177/1609406919840516

This research examines how interviewers' questions and expressions encourage or inhibit children from telling their stories.

7

RESEARCH WITH ADULTS

════════════ Chapter Aims ════════════

This chapter will explore the following common data collection methods, and features of research with adults, with advice on each:

- Interviewing adults;
- Observing teaching;
- Tasks;
- Surveys and questionnaires;
- Examples of research projects which utilised quantitative methods;
- Recruiting/selecting adults;
- Incentives;
- Involving parents (not advised).

INTRODUCTION

It is highly likely that your research project will involve adults who work in the school(s) or setting(s) that you are familiar with. You are, therefore, likely to have at least a distant professional relationship with each of them. This is not a problem in itself. It does not diminish the validity of your study, or constitute a conflict of interest, but it should be acknowledged in your methodology chapter so that you demonstrate your awareness of power dynamics and bias. The most common methods students have used with adults in the research projects we have supervised are interviews, observations, tasks and surveys or questionnaires (not both), and this chapter will explore each in turn.

INTERVIEWING ADULTS

Whereas it is advisable from a safeguarding point of view to interview children in groups, it is likely that you will interview adults individually, not least because people who work in schools are very busy and trying to find a time when more than one person is available is very hard. Also, many adults prefer to be interviewed individually.

Be very aware that the time the teachers or Learning Support Assistants (LSAs) give you is precious. Sometimes the only time you can both meet is snatched from an already packed timetable, so do not expect an extended 45-minute time of considered and luxuriated reflection. Yes, you can bring tea and biscuits. Yes, you want to ease your participant into the interview with some gentle easy questions to contextualise your focus, but do not waste time with questions that are not directly relevant to your study. Fortunately, teachers tend to be extremely skilled at moving immediately and seamlessly from one situation to another (perhaps teaching chemistry to a difficult Year 8 class, then straight into PSHE lesson with Year 10, followed by a meeting with the science team, then an interview with you, before a Teams meeting with a parent). Be mindful of your participants' needs and be sure to thank them.

Having said that, do not feel you are intruding or getting in their way. They will be very pleased to help you, and they will be interested in your study (or they would not have offered). They genuinely want to be involved, but you must help them by being concise, open-minded, clear in your questions or scenarios, a good listener, and very well organised (you are punctual, and all your resources are present and working).

THE DESIGN OF YOUR QUESTIONS

The chapter on methodology (see Chapter 6) explores the design of interviews in terms of structured, unstructured or semi-structured interviews, but here we explore the structure of the questions themselves. This is vital if you are to conduct an effective interview which generates rich and useful data. It is very common amongst students to give insufficient thought to how they intend to phrase questions, and if questions are clumsy this can at best lead to the collection of poor, uninteresting data, and at worst to the causing of offence.

You are already aware from your initial teacher training course of the value of open questions in developing discussion amongst children in the classroom. The same is true in research interviews of course, but there is an additional skill here. In your day-to-day teaching in the classroom, you might want to direct children to a particular line of thought through your open questions. In an interview for a research project, you absolutely do not. You are looking to discover the participants' views, not to confirm your own preconceptions, or pushing participants along a pre-planned line of enquiry. Your questions must not direct or lead a participant or suggest a right or wrong (or preferred) answer.

This can be quite nuanced. For example, when questioning teachers or LSAs, the question 'What do you feel are the most important features of a role play area?' is a much better question than 'What are the most important features of a role play area?' In the first question you are exploring only this one teacher's perceptions, and you are giving your participant freedom to express anything they choose to. By contrast, the second question subtly suggests that the interviewee really ought to know and share views with every other teacher about role play areas, and this immediately puts a little pressure on your participant to tell you the right answer. They may wonder whether they have told you the right thing. Then, having negotiated this question, the participant will be a little apprehensive about your next one, and the interview starts to spiral down into cautious responses and short answers.

As other examples, consider the experiences of the participants if asked these similarly sounding questions (see Table 7.1).

Table 7.1 Examples of Similar Sounding Questions

Question Set 1	Question Set 2
What is the most effective way of arranging furniture in a classroom?	Tell me why you have the tables and chairs arranged the way you do?
Tell me about the school policy on marking children's work?	What are your priorities when marking children's work?
Why is it important to welcome children when they come into the classroom?	I am interested in the way you welcome children when they come into the classroom. Tell me about that please.
What works best in behaviour management in a Reception setting?	From your own experience, what advice would you give to an Early Career Teacher about behaviour management in this Reception setting?

In all these examples, by asking the second question, you are making the interviewee the expert, and you are setting the parameters of the interview around the teacher's experiences, practices, and attitudes. But if you choose instead to ask the first question, you are making the interviewee a spokesperson for all teachers everywhere, or for other teachers in the school, and in doing so you have set the parameters very much wider. To answer the first question, the teacher has to look beyond their own practice to find the norms or best practice of the profession generally. Obviously, this will serve to make the teacher uncomfortable, and they may start to look at their watch and wonder whether they really ought to be preparing for that online meeting with the parent, which is the next thing in their diary, and which suddenly looks a much more attractive option than this rather difficult interview.

Phrasing of Questions That You Should Avoid

There are questions which you absolutely must avoid: namely those that are likely to prompt a participant into criticising the school or naming other people. Asking such questions is easily done if you are not careful, but innocent sounding questions can lead to very unexpected and negative responses. You should not feel as if you have done something wrong if some negativity spontaneously arises in the questions that you ask because this can happen, but equally, as with Emanuel's experience in Chapter 4 (Ethics), you should not be fishing for negativity either.

If negative responses do arise you would be wise not to report them in your data analysis for ethical reasons. The school would not be happy if, having given you permission to undertake research, you end up encouraging participants to criticise the school's processes, procedures, personnel, or resources, even if everything is kept anonymous.

Examples of the types of wording in questions we advise you to avoid are:

- How helpful is the school policy on ...
- What might the school do differently about ...
- Are you happy with the way ...
- What are the biggest problems you experience with ...
- How realistic is ...
- Do you have strong views about ...

And you must not, of course, ask questions which could identify anyone in the school (for example 'How do you accommodate Felicity's special needs?'). This is true even if you think those who are named will be pleased with what is said (for example 'Who are the most creative teachers in this school?').

Observing Teaching

Observation of teaching sounds like a very good way of triangulating a research question, and it can be. That said, you must be very careful here (ethics again). For example, when planning her study, Claire intends to first interview Key Stage 2 teachers about how they maintain the pace of lessons and then observe their teaching to see the effect these strategies have. She might do this the other way round by observing lessons and then afterwards asking teachers about interesting things that she noticed. She has not decided which way round yet. She will ask her supervisor.

▬▬▬▬ Reflective Questions 7.1 ▬▬▬▬

Claire could not see any significant ethical issues here, but she was surprised that even at the ethics proposal stage, her supervisor vetoed these observations, on ethical grounds. Can you suggest why?

The supervisor asked Claire to think again because there is a big difference between observations of teachers where the children are active participants in what the teacher or TA is doing, and where the children are passive recipients of the teacher's practice. Let's separate these out.

Observations of Teachers Where the Children Are Active Participants

Observations of teachers or TAs in classrooms almost never happen without children in the classroom, and if children are actively involved in what is being observed, then they are, by definition, part of the observation. From an ethical point of view, you will therefore need their permission, and the permission of their parents.

Claire wants to explore ways in which teachers in Key Stage 2 maintain the pace of lessons when children are undertaking individual tasks at their desks. Mrs Allen is a Year 3 teacher in Claire's study, and in an interview undertaken before the lesson she has told

Claire that she (Mrs Allen) is very mobile in the classroom, even when the children are working at their desks, and that although she is mainly focused on a particular group for assessment purposes, she likes to keep moving and to parachute randomly and spontaneously into the progress and activities of other tables. Claire is fascinated to see this strategy in action, particularly the way Mrs Allen engages with the 'slow coaches' as she sometimes calls them (to their faces, which Claire is not sure about, but the children don't seem to mind). Claire is struck both by the strategy of seemingly random visits to tables, and by the animated way Mrs Allen engages with the children. They clearly love her.

You will agree, we hope, that Claire's is not an isolated observation of a teacher. This is an observation of a relationship. The children are busy (but often not busy enough, in Mrs Allen's opinion). Their busy-ness, or lack of it, attracts a response from her. Since there are multiple players in this situation, multiple permissions are needed, even if Claire is only interested in one side of this relationship. The ethics here are complex, and so the ethics committee must have a view, and are likely to have a say.

In your head (or even out loud) you may now be shouting at this book on Claire's behalf, and railing against the supervisor or ethics committee. 'Agh'. you are exclaiming, 'Ethics is such a pain. All it does is serve to get in the way of perfectly harmless research ideas. Who is going to get hurt by Claire observing a teacher who chooses to be mobile around a classroom? Nobody, that's who! The members of the ethics committee clearly do not have enough to do if they are so fixated on stuff like this'. We have heard these sentiments from student teachers many times.

The writers of this book are both members of ethics committees, and in our defense, we reiterate here the point we made in Chapter 4 (Ethics). In your school placement, no one is stopping you from observing teachers' interactions with children, and by so doing, improving your own professional practice. But your role as a researcher comes with different rules and responsibilities from your role as a teacher. To secure a very good grade in your research project, the most important thing is not demonstrating that you have found a positive answer to your research question. The most important thing is to demonstrate your ability to undertake a valid and ethically sound piece of research. You must therefore demonstrate to your marker why you have done what you have done, and perhaps, why you chose not to do things that might, on the face of it, have seemed a good idea. The bottom line, since you are reading this book to be successful in your research project, is that ethically sound research practice gets you a better grade. Practice which is ethically suspect will cost you marks, and rightly so. Now, are you still railing against the ethics committee for vetoing your ethically unsound suggestion and stopping you doing something which could negatively affect your degree classification? We hope not.

Two Examples of Observations of Teachers Where the Children Are Passive to Your Research Focus

If the children are passive in terms of your research, then you are much safer when observing teachers or teaching assistants (TAs). Here are two examples of such situations.

Observation Example 1

You are interested in the way teachers give instructions, so you observe them during lesson introductions and plenaries. This could be applicable in any year group or Key Stage. Your focus is likely to be on the vocabulary teachers use; on the complexity of the instructions; the specificity of instructions; the way teachers check to see if the instructions have been understood; the incidence of repetition; the extent to which teachers use modelling to the children to show them what success would look like, and the methods they used in their modelling. Here you are observing only the teacher's performance and techniques. It is highly unlikely that the children will have a direct impact upon important features of the teachers' practice that you are focusing on, even though the children are engaged in the lesson. Their behaviour or responses are not integral to the observation, as those of the children in Mrs Allen's class had been. You are not observing a relationship, so your supervisor and the ethics committee will not hold strong views.

Observation Example 2

You are interested in the perceptions of Key Stage 2 teachers and TAs regarding their experiences of play-time duty, and the strategies they adopt. You may decide to interview them as well as observe them on duty to get a sense of real-time events which can be commented on or discussed. For example, you notice in the observation that Mr Hewitt likes to be hands-on with children in the playground, particularly those who are likely to be disruptive. In an interview he discloses that his strategy is to prevent problems by being where they are most likely to happen. Miss Gupta, by contrast, walks around the outside of the playground surveying it constantly. She points out in the interview that she is never in the middle because that would mean she would have her back to half of the playground all the time. Mrs Ellard tends to be static. She has a particular place near the edge of the playground that she stands in. This is because she has a good line of sight of the whole playground, the children know where she is, and she likes to stay in the sunshine.

You are safe to observe teachers in this setting because the children will be running around, or playing games, or just standing and chatting, and the teachers or TAs will be monitoring them. As with example 1, the children are not integral to the observation. The children are not directly contributing to the behaviours of the people being observed.

THE USE OF TASKS

We briefly identified in Chapter 3 (Types of Research) aspects of inviting participants to engage in tasks, for example the keeping of a diary, sorting activities, drawing, surveys and questionnaires, and we explore the logistics of these further in Chapter 8 (A chapter of case studies). All these data collection tools are suitable in different ways for adults and children, but here we consider the use of tasks specifically for adult participants.

You should not feel that gathering data by giving adults tasks to do is in some way patronising or not worthy of their time. They are likely to be intrigued or pleased it is not 'only an interview'. But before we give examples where tasks have been applied successfully in projects we have overseen, here is an example of what appears to be a simple sorting activity which promises much but would almost certainly deliver very little in terms of data. We will explore the logistics of this task once you have engaged with it.

Activity 7.1

You have agreed to participate in a piece of research that the writers of this book are undertaking. Our research title is *'What preferences are held by student teacher researchers regarding the tasks that participants are asked to do?'* You have been invited to put the following activities in order of your preference of tasks you might hope to do as a participant in a piece of research. If you cannot put them in a linear order, you can have a diamond shape if you prefer. You are asked to rank all 12.

- A 30-minute interview.
- A 45-minute interview.
- Individually sorting eight to ten statements in order of your priority or into categories, and explaining your choices to the researcher as you go along.
- In a group, sorting 8-10 statements in order of your priority or into categories, observed by the researcher.
- Keeping a daily or weekly diary.
- Having your professional practice observed.
- Taking photographs of significant areas of aspects of your classroom or school (no children, obviously).
- Taking a walk with the researcher around significant areas of your classroom or school which are significant to you, and talking about them.
- Doing an online questionnaire (multiple choice mainly).
- Doing an online survey (mixture of multiple choice and text comments).
- Making a timeline (online or in hard copy) of significant professional experiences you have had over the last five or ten years.
- Drawing in hard copy a collection of significant professional experiences you have had over the last 5 or 10 years.

Let's explore how effective that task was for the purposes of informing our research question. On the face of it, it looked as if it was going to be a good one, but you have probably realised already that it was not. It is highly likely that you struggled to arrange all twelve (because there are too many statements) or you simply chose not to do the task at all because ordering twelve statements or options is a big ask, or you started and then lost motivation, or you became bored or annoyed. You were not patronised by being asked to do the task, but you did not enjoy it because it was too big, and as a result you probably did not complete it. This would be a very bad situation for us as researchers, because the data we hoped for is not going to be forthcoming, but it is entirely our own fault.

You must therefore bear that experience in mind when deciding upon tasks for adults. In doing that previous task you would have almost certainly preferred to be asked to choose just your top two or three options, and at a push, identify your two least favourite options. That would have been a manageable task which you would have seen through to completion, and even though you were given the same menu of twelve statements, that smaller activity would have successfully and clearly identified your main preferences to us. The data you gave us would have strongly contributed to informing our research question. A clear pattern of preferences would be identifiable when we analysed responses from across the cohort of participants.

In the original task there is no benefit to us as the researchers in discovering that your seventh favourite option, from a menu of 12, is keeping a diary. No, we want headlines from each participant. We want participants to complete tasks, and to enjoy them. If it was essential to our research question that we needed all statements ordered, we should have given you five statements at most.

Had that task (to sort all 12) been given to even a large cohort of participating students, very little usable data would have been generated. Most participating students would have at best lost interest, probably placing options randomly just to make the task stop by completing it thoughtlessly, or at worst they would withdraw. All this would have happened because we had not thought through what data it was essential for us to gather, and what the experience of the participants would be.

Tasks can therefore be very good generators of interesting data, and we recommend their use, but you must know clearly what the task is seeking to achieve, what the data it generates will look like, how useful that data will be for you, and what the experience of the participants will be. A pilot is always a good idea (where you try out the design of your study on willing volunteers, to check that it works and the quality of data it produces).

Here are some examples of tasks that have worked well in research projects we have supervised, and we also include one example that did not.

Task Example 1: Keeping a Diary

Meg was a science trainee in a secondary school in Durham. Very shortly before Meg arrived, the school had introduced a new virtual learning environment (VLE) where, amongst other things, pupils could store their work, undertake projects, upload homework and engage in group chats. The VLE also monitored pupils' attendance in school and their engagement with the VLE itself. Meg was fascinated by the VLE, but she was a bit overwhelmed by it, so she wanted to explore the teachers' use of it, and to hear their views about it. Rather than just interviewing the teachers, Meg asked as many teachers as were willing, from any department, to keep a brief diary for a fortnight, just identifying how they had used the VLE, and their attitudes towards it in terms of that day's activity, and generally. Nine teachers signed up (Meg was hoping for more).

Most of the 9 were faithful to the diary on most days, and diary entries were predominantly positive. Meg discovered some uses for the VLE that she had not previously thought of (such as children engaging in non-synchronous tasks), but she discovered that the teachers enjoyed keeping the diaries, as it gave them an arena in which they could condense their thoughts about the VLE. Meg knows this because afterwards she organised two separate group interviews, one of which six of the nine teachers were able to attend, where they shared their views on the VLE. Meg was surprised and delighted when the conversation in the second interview (three teachers) spontaneously moved to the teachers' positive experiences of keeping the diary. This was an unexpected bonus, and Meg chose to briefly report their attitudes in a separate section of her data analysis chapter.

Diaries are not always a good choice of data collection tool, however. For example, Vivian was in a primary school that had a forest school area. He was intrigued by it and developed an interest in outdoor learning. He then found that six teachers were taking 60 Year 2 children (in two separate classes of 30) on a residential trip to an outdoor centre in Kent. One class of children were to be there from Monday to Wednesday: the second from Wednesday to Friday. Vivian hoped to go, but he was not teaching Year 2 and so was not part of the trip. Instead, he asked the six teachers to keep a diary, cataloguing their key thoughts and experiences each day. The teachers agreed to do so. Vivian also intended to interview some of the children on their return about their learning experiences. On their return from the trip, four of the six teachers made a diary entry on the Monday. One did on the Tuesday. No entries were completed after that. Anyone who has ever taken children on a residential school trip will be unsurprised by this, since the writing of a diary is a very low priority when you are deep in the Kent countryside and responsible for thirty Year 2 children's safety, hygiene, and whereabouts.

Task Example 2: Two Ways of Ranking Statements, and the Benefits of a Pilot

So Vivian abandoned his residential diary idea. Instead, he opted for a simple study of teachers' perceptions of Forest School learning. He decided to present participant teachers and Learning Support Assistants from across the school with written statements about aspects of outdoor learning and teaching, drawn from his observation of teachers in the forest school area. Vivian was undecided whether to offer the teachers approximately twelve statements and ask them to identify the extent to which they agreed or disagreed with each using a Likert scale, or whether to give them five or six statements and ask the participants to rank them in priority. In a decision which Vivian realised in hindsight improved his research project no end, he did a pilot. He asked five fellow students to trial both. They quite enjoyed the Likert scales approach; they suggested some changes to the wording of some of the statements; and each took between four to seven minutes to complete the task. Their responses showed some variation. The fellow students also quite enjoyed the five-statement sorting exercise, but did not suggest changes to the wording, and each completed the task in less than two minutes. There was very little variation in their completed lists, in fact three were identical. Armed with these outcomes, because of the lack of variation in the sorting exercise responses, Vivian decided to go with the 12 statements using the Likert scale option.

Vivian had devised the initial 12 statements himself, but because he was in a rush to collect data for this new focus after the failure of his diary idea, he had not given himself time to read very widely around the subject, and the statements he gave his participants, who were not fellow students as in the pilot but instead were experienced forest school practitioners, lacked insight or breadth for them. As a result, although his method was theoretically sound, and his use of a pilot had informed and strengthened his method (and impressed his markers), the data he collected was predictable, and so its analysis was rather uninspiring. Vivian's final grade was 62%, which was lower than his average for the rest of the year, but a lot better than he had feared when his diary idea had proved ill-considered.

Vivian got together with five other students one weekend to pilot each of their data collection ideas. Most tested interview questions. Some brought tasks. Some went on to borrow each other's ideas. All six students benefitted enormously from doing this, as their data collection tools were improved markedly, and they gained a great deal of confidence from having other students test their ideas and methods. Might you consider doing this with some of your fellow students?

Task Example 3: Q-Sort, and an Unexpected Benefit of Using Artificial Intelligence to Help Plan Your Study

The sorting activity that Vivian wisely rejected from his research project was a rudimentary form of Q-sort methodology, in which participants prioritise given statements, usually into a pyramid formation. Vivian's mistake was to generate these statements himself, thus limiting the scope of the statements to his own attitudes, preconceptions, and experience, all of which were limited.

By contrast, Ashley, a primary trainee in Birmingham, had heard of Q-sort through a piece of research that one of her lecturers was doing, and she was intrigued by it. Her lecturer, Adam, was exploring ways schools use their facilities for commercial use and the diverse positive and challenging impacts this might have on the school environment. Adam had interviewed 15 participants from four local schools and had gone on to select the statements from both majority and minority responses from these interviews. He had then made the sorting activity available online using licenced software, and using his national networking channels had recruited over one hundred participants, thus generating a huge amount of workable data, designed to identify the extent to which a large cohort of interested teachers supported the arguments made in the interviews, and to validate the responses (or not). Ashley thought this was a brilliant way of collecting qualitative data, but how was she to arrange for participants to sort the statements when she had neither access to licenced software nor a national networking channel, and how was she to generate the statements other than by making them up herself? Her supervisor suggested that for the sorting, Ashley simply recruit participants from schools she has connections with, asking them to sort statements that Ashley had written on separate flash cards, to photograph the results, and to send the photos to her. For the statements, Ashley was amazed when her supervisor suggested she used artificial intelligence. Using her university's preferred AI assistant, (on this occasion, Microsoft Copilot), Ashley typed in 'Statements about teaching touch typing or handwriting in primary schools' and she was presented with five arguments which were positive about learning touch typing, four arguments which were positive about handwriting, and four that were balanced. Ashley could easily turn these arguments into statements. She had to adapt the arguments to turn them into statements because they were a bit long, but this process made Ashley realise that if she was faithful to the suggestions made by Copilot, her own prejudices were, if not irradicated, certainly less obvious. Prior to this, Ashley thought teaching handwriting in a digital world was at best anachronistic, and at worst a complete waste of time, but seeing the AI-generated arguments which celebrated the teaching and use of handwriting (cognitive benefits, fine motor skill development, enhanced spelling and reading skills, deeper cognitive processing) made her take a much broader approach to her research question than she had considered up to that point. She felt that her submission was so much stronger as a result of using AI in this way, because initially she had been trying to make an academically supported argument against the teaching of paper-based writing skills, thinking herself to be forward thinking. Her research project had broadened her attitudes and perspectives.

The use of artificial intelligence is also considered in Chapter 4 of this book (Ethics).

EXAMPLES OF RESEARCH PROJECTS WHICH UTILISED QUANTITATIVE METHODS

Most research projects that we have supported have involved the use of exclusively qualitative methods, but a significant minority of students do choose to incorporate quantitative data collection methods. The reasons that students choose to include a quantitative element end to fall into three camps: the first two positive, the third less so.

1 Students come from a science, technical, engineering, or mathematical background, and they feel either safe, comfortable or compelled to use this approach.
2 Students want to demonstrate clear triangulation and want to use mixed methods to achieve this.
3 Students see research in terms of having to prove something, and therefore they wrongly consider that only a pursuit of objective reality will do (see Chapter 2).

It would be wrong of us as supervisors to veto an intention to use quantitative approaches, but if you are considering using quantitative methods, please be advised that for a research project there is no need go to extreme lengths to justify it, or to analyse your data as if you were writing for a four-star international science journal. We have seen research project proposals that refer to the student's intention to undertake regression analysis, or to use Statistical Package for the Social Sciences software (SPSS), so that they might be able to demonstrate statistical significance. All of this is unnecessary. There is no need to employ correlation analysis, t-tests, or non-probability sampling. You do not need to secure a representative sample sufficient to achieve an impressive calculated statistical power. We have seen all of these in proposals. No. Instead, if you choose to collect quantitative data, all you need do is explain why this approach is appropriate for your research question, and if your supervisor agrees that the approach is appropriate, to present the findings in a clear way, probably using simple tables, graphs and charts.

Be strongly advised, however, that if you choose to collect quantitative data through surveys or questionaries, you must be certain to allow participants the space to offer perceptions or observations as well. We have all participated in questionnaires where the given options did not match our experiences, and so we struggled to give an accurate response, or gave no response at all. You must try to avoid giving your participants that experience.

We include here five examples of studies where quantitative data has been collected: four of them to good effect, one poorly administered. None of these studies was exclusively quantitative in nature – each collected qualitative data too. Most used Likert scales, but we hope you will find it interesting to read the range of research questions that lent themselves to a quantitative element.

Quantitative Example 1

Eve was interested in the use of Makaton in Key Stage 3 and 4 classrooms across a range of subjects, both its frequency of use, and the extent to which the signs and symbols were the primary use of communication or whether they were used to support spoken language or other communication use. She included appropriate multiple-choice questions in a questionnaire which produced quantitative data (How frequently do you use Makaton in your classroom? In which of these following situations do you use Makaton?) and she used Likert scales (for example, To what extent do you agree with the following statement, 'The use of Makaton benefits the whole class, not just those for whom its use is intended and tailored'). Eve was worried that there would be situations in which secondary teachers used Makaton that she had not thought to include in the questionnaire, and so she built in opportunities within it for teachers to offer additional responses, which she could add to her tallies if necessary.

Quantitative Example 2

Kurumi was a PGCE secondary student, teaching French and Spanish, undertaking her research project immediately after her final placement. During her first school placement in a different school, a Year 10 child died in a road accident, an incident which created huge emotional reactions throughout the school. Her research project proposal was entitled *What types of training are typically available for teachers and trainee teachers regarding giving support to bereaved children?* We did explore with Kurumi whether this was a wise choice of focus given the experience that she had had, but she was adamant that this was where her interest wanted to go. We allowed it, but together with Kurumi we agreed that for purposes of mental and emotional well-being, both Kurumi's and of the teachers who agreed to participate, she would not interview anyone. Rather, she would explore school and education authority policies, guidelines and documentation, present UK child-mortality statistics (from accidents, disease, conditions, murders, and suicides) and she would develop a questionnaire for teachers which included the use of Likert scales (for example 'How important do you think it is for teachers to have access to CPD on supporting childhood bereavement?'). Eve was able to recruit participants from three separate schools, including the one where she undertook her first placement, and the difference in responses (and recruitment numbers) from the different schools was remarkable. The disproportionately high number of participants from her first placement school was a finding in itself.

Quantitative Example 3

What is 'Possibility Thinking', in what Key Stage 1 and 2 subjects can it be applied, and how can the practice of Teacher-in-Role encourage it? Neil, a Primary teacher trainee, used this rather convoluted but self-explanatory title for his research project. He knew which techniques were commonly used in the school from conversations and observation of other teachers before designing his questionnaire, and from this, he was able to catalogue the ways in which participating teachers who employed Teacher-in-Role practice applied it, and to identify and order which techniques were most popular by frequency of use (hot seating, the 'what-if' hat, freeze frames, role play), which he presented in a pie chart. He listed and tallied the subjects in which teachers had said they used Teacher-in-Role and found that across his participant cohort of six teachers, every curriculum area was deemed appropriate for 'what-if' questions by at least one of them, and he presented the tally in a bar chart. Neil tallied the number of times different types of barriers to using drama techniques were mentioned by the teachers when he interviewed them (confidence of children, resources, lack of assessment opportunities), and compared the different tallies between Key Stage 1 and Key Stage 2.

This all looks at first glance to be very impressive, compelling and attractive, but it must be said that Neil completely overdid it with his analysis of the quantitative data, and this negatively affected his overall grade. For example, only one teacher said she had recently used role play as the Teacher-in Role (when showing children a flat iron during a lesson on the Victorians), yet Neil had presented that single use as a percentage. Similarly, there were not enough teachers in his cohort to compare Key Stage 1 responses with those from Key Stage 2 with any sense of granularity, but Neil did this anyway. Many responses from the teachers were unique to each teacher yet were analysed by counting them against the equally peculiar responses of all the other teachers. That is very poor quantitative analysis. Neil's initial quantitative analysis of the data in which all teachers shared at least similar experiences, such as their frequency of use of common techniques, was appropriate. Neil was so pleased with his initial charts and graphs, however, he did not know when to stop. If you are considering quantitative aspects for your research project, please learn from Neil. Quantitative analysis of small amounts of data or from a small number of participants demonstrates to your marker a clear lack of understanding about what quantitative analysis can do and when its use is appropriate.

Quantitative Example 4

By contrast, Xavier's research project title was *Primary school teachers' responses to Mind-fulness activities*. Examples of Likert scale statements were 'I enjoy Mindfulness activities', 'Mindfulness helps me moderate my emotions when things are getting frustrating in school', and 'I can practice mindfulness in school'. Xavier used quantitative data very sparingly, and to good effect. He used it only to inform and supplement the interviews he conducted with teachers, and it added well-observed breadth to his study.

Quantitative Example 5

Anna-Maria, undertaking her final teacher training placement in a Year 4 class, was interested in provision for pupils with SEND, particularly children with dyscalculia. Like Neil above, she designed her questionnaire in a way that enabled her to easily recognise data that could be analysed quantitatively, but unlike Neil, she did not analyse the data to death. For example, Anna-Maria asked 'Please identify any support strategies you have used for children who have been identified with a special need or disability', and she tallied the responses. Later in the questionnaire she would ask specifically about dyscalculia. Some of the most interesting responses came from a three-option multiple-choice question quite late in the questionnaire, which was a question from which the responses could be tallied – 'Are the support strategies you use aimed pre-dominantly at minimising unwanted behaviours, improving academic outcomes, or both'. To convert this quantitative question to a qualitative one, in the subsequent question Anna-Maria asked, 'If you can, please expand on your answer to the previous question'. The first was a question that gave many teachers pause for thought, and this came out in their responses to the second. Anna-Maria was able to explore this more fully in later interviews with some of the participants. The original multiple-choice question, which had been presented to be analysed in a quantitative format, went on to generate rich qualitative data.

RECRUITING/SELECTING ADULTS

There is a knack to this. If you are looking to interview participants, many students simply approach potential participants in a rather cold-calling way and ask for participation ("I have to do a research project for my course. Would you mind if I interviewed you? It is about children's perceptions of historical timelines,"). In this scenario, the potential participant is made to feel to be a means to an end, and the research project is portrayed as a rather inconvenient hoop for you to jump through to get your qualification, and participants are left wondering what a historical timeline might encompass. Far better to bring up the topic of your research first, perhaps in the staff room. If you tell people about your interest in the topic, it is highly likely that they will be interested too. Once you have kindled their interest or identified to yourself who is and who is not interested, you will be much more successful in getting a positive response to your request to take part, and people will feel motivated to help you. If you are lucky, you might even generate some discussion about your intended topic (which you cannot use directly as data, but it may give you additional preliminary ideas about how others think about it, and this could inform your questions, or alter your research question).

You will need written consent from all participants. Below is a typical consent form.

Information and Consent Sheet for Adult Participants

Who Is This Information Sheet For?

This information sheet is for ...... [teachers, TAs] who are interested in participating in a research project.

We would like *you/your staff/your pupils/your child* to be invited to be involved a research project [Put the title of your research project here]

Before you decide whether you want to take part, it is important for you to understand why the research project is being done and what your participation will involve.

Please take the time to read the following information carefully. Please take the time to decide whether you wish to take part.

What Is the Purpose of the Project?

The project aims to explore...................... [put the brief information from the proposal here.]

Why Have I Been Chosen?

You are being invited to take part in this project because you are in a good position about your experiences within education to provide information regarding the project.

What Will Participation Involve?

I shall be asking you to............ [engage in interview or questionnaires or observation etc.]

As part of the presentation of results, your own words may be used in text form. This will be anonymised, so that you cannot be identified from what you said. All the research data will be stored as hard copy or electronic copy in a secure password protected computer or on a cloud-based system (as applicable).

Please note that:

- Participants can decide to stop the research process at any point.
- Participants need not answer questions that they do not wish to.
- Names will be removed from the information and anonymised. It should not be possible to identify anyone from my reports on this project.

(Continued)

(Continued)

It is up to participants to decide whether to take part or not. If you decide to take part, you are still free to withdraw any time up until DD/MM/YYYY (and beyond providing contact is made with the researcher) and without giving a reason. If you withdraw from the project, all data will be withdrawn and deleted.

- I have read the information sheet about this project.
- I have had an opportunity to ask questions and discuss this project.
- I have received satisfactory answers to all my questions.
- I have received enough information about this project.
- I understand that I am/the participant (s) is/are free to withdraw from this project:
  ○ At any time (until such date as this will no longer be possible, which I have been told).
  ○ Without giving a reason for withdrawing.
  ○ My data will be stored securely.
- I agree to take part in this project.

Signed (participant):
  Date:
  Name in block letters:
  Signature of researcher:
  Date:
  This project is supervised by:
  Researcher's main supervisor's contact details:

Incentives

This was raised in the scenarios we presented in Chapter 4 (Ethics). Extreme caution needs to be exercised here. The British Educational Research Association (BERA) (2024) guidance (number 33) reads *'Researchers' use of incentives to encourage participation should be commensurate with good sense, such that the level of incentive does not impinge on the free decision to participate. The use of incentives should be acknowledged in any reporting of the research.'* We would not recommend any use of an incentive in your research project, but we know that in return for participation, students have offered to cover such things as playground duties or other supervision roles. One secondary student offered to do additional marking for several teachers and very much regretted it once the scale of the task became apparent. To offer incentives is to buy participation, and if it is put like that, you can see that the likelihood of social desirability bias and the Hawthorne effect (Chapter 6) is heavily raised. Our strong advice is that you should not consider offering incentives to participants of your research project. You enter murky waters, ethically and professionally, if you do so.

Involving Parents (Also Not Advised)

We do not advise you to involve parents in your research project. Their involvement introduces many unknown and potentially dangerous variables to your work. Inexperienced researchers often see parents as an interesting source of triangulation, since parents will hold alternative perspectives and viewpoints to teachers about the education of children. This is certainly true. But of course, unlike the teacher, the parent is not all that interested in the education of children. They are mainly interested in the education of their own child. It is perhaps possible that a parent who offers to take part in your study may be 100% supportive of the school, entirely happy with their child's education experience and progress, and they value every teacher in the school equally. Alternatively, at the other end of the scale, a parent may hold a grudge against the school or a particular teacher, in which case they will see your research project as a mouthpiece to articulate their frustrations. If you invited, say, six parents to answer questions about something as innocuous as school uniform, at least one of them will give you data you won't feel able to report because it is critical of the school, and if you interviewed the six of them together in a group, the criticisms of the school could easily escalate amongst them ('Do you know, you're right. I'd not seen that before. It is a rubbish uniform'), and before you know it the head teacher is receiving complaints or suggestions about how the uniform or policy could be changed, or the deputy head has become suddenly aware of disparaging remarks about the school uniform on social media.

And what research question could you ask that compellingly needed the involvement of parents? Perhaps their experiences of getting their children to school might be explored because in that at least they are the experts, but we doubt very much that this is a question that interests you. You certainly would not want to ask about the communication that they receive from the school – that would just be asking for trouble. Knowingly or inadvertently, when you involve parents in your research you are in danger of generating criticism of the school. That is why Ofsted always survey parents when they undertake an inspection. Do not go there.

SUMMARY

The main messages we hope you take from this chapter are:

- When devising question for participants about their perceptions, be sure to couch them around only the views or experiences of the participant. Do not make the participant feel they must be a mouthpiece for the whole profession.
- Do not fish for responses that might be critical of the participant's school, or that one might anticipate would lead to a participant becoming angry or frustrated.
- Be very clear in your own mind who and what you are observing if you engage in observations. In a classroom situation, is it possible to only observe the teacher? Your parameters and intentions must be clear before you start.
- Tasks can be a really effective way of collecting data and engaging with participants, but be sure to pilot them first, to make sure they are fit for purpose, enjoyable, and that they generate suitable data.
- There is a knack to securing participants which involves demonstrating your interest in the subject and kindling theirs before asking the can-I-interview-you question.
- We do not recommend involving parents in your research.

FURTHER READING

British Educational Research Association (BERA) (2024). *Ethical guidelines for educational research*, 5th edn. [Online] Available at: https://www.bera.ac.uk/publication/ethical-guidelines-for-educational-research-fifth-edition-2024-online (accessed: January 2025).

The intended audience for these guidelines is anyone undertaking educational research – whether their job description includes research, or they conduct research within the field (for example, while studying for a qualification or with the intention of improving practice). This includes both independent researchers and practitioners based in educational institutions of any kind.

Malpass, A., Breel, A., Stubbs, J. et al. (2023). 'Create to collaborate: Using creative activity and participatory performance in online workshops to build collaborative research relationships' *Research Involvement and Engagement* 9, 111 (2023). https://doi.org/10.1186/s40900-023-00512-8

Create to Collaborate aimed to develop and facilitate creative public involvement workshops with members of the public, researchers, and community organisations, who were potentially interested in collaborating on a future health research project.

8
EQUALITY, DIVERSITY AND INCLUSION: A CHAPTER OF RELATED CASE STUDIES

━━━━━━━━━ Chapter Aims ━━━━━━━━━

- To explore ways to make your research project inclusive – implications and complications of a commitment to Equality, Diversity and Inclusion (EDI), with a case study.
- To present overviews of a series of research project examples, which present both successes and cautionary tales.
- To broaden your consideration of what might be possible or desirable in your choice of data collection tools.
- To identify situations in which your chosen research tool might serve to restrict the quality or quantity of your research data.

INTRODUCTION

This chapter contains a series of summaries of previous students' research projects, and some of the issues that arose along the way. The first of the examples we give concerns EDI, which comes with its own specific implications, and so that area of research has been amplified in this chapter before and after the example. All the examples we give here were successful on first submission (with different degrees of success), but all these projects contain aspects which developed problems, often in ways that the student had not foreseen. In all cases we celebrate the aspects of each project which promised much, but we also identify any significant unexpected factors that arose, or what went wrong, or errors that the students made which in hindsight they wish they had not. There is no such thing as the perfect research project, but this chapter is included so that you might learn from the mistakes of those that have gone before you, or sympathise with their misfortune. Consequently, we hope you might be forearmed, and more diligent and wary than they were when approaching unforeseen or hidden pitfalls that may lurk in your path. Please be aware that these examples are not typical. It is not the case that all students have the sort of experiences that we report here. These examples are uncommon, but each highlight in one way or another the sorts of thing that can arise if you are not careful (and sometimes even if you are).

MAKING YOUR RESEARCH PROJECT INCLUSIVE: THE IMPLICATIONS AND COMPLICATIONS OF A COMMITMENT TO EDI, WITH AN EXAMPLE

There can be unexpected tensions when considering EDI within your research project. If insensitively done, your commitment to EDI can unhelpfully influence your research project methods. Both writers of this book encourage research students to practice inclusive research methods, but this can be an unexpectedly tricky arena. A significant minority of students who we have supported start the process with an impressive degree of ambition about EDI in their research project, but often this commitment is either unhelpful, unrealistic or even counterproductive. Sometimes, and always reluctantly, we have had to rein students in for the purposes of their assessed submission. Let us explain.

Your ambition regarding inclusivity is likely to fall somewhere along a line between two points. At one end of the scale, even though you are committed to EDI, you may want to do no more than ensure that your research design is accessible to all potential participants, irrespective of their background, culture, identity, and circumstances. You have no specific agenda for inclusion within your project other than to avoid doing or planning anything which could lead to any participant feeling excluded, uncomfortable, upset, or isolated. That is a perfectly acceptable approach to take, and the majority of students hold an approximation of that position. First and foremost, do no harm. But many students want to do more than that. At the other end of the scale, there are students who, from the very outset, aim to use their research project to champion the needs of a disadvantaged minority. We know from experience that many students may be (for example) ardent feminists or perhaps they are committed advocates of Marxist theory or Critical Race Theory. If you are numbered amongst these students (and thank you if that is the case, because right now our society needs people who are passionate and vocal about social justice), you might be tempted to use your research project to call out political oppression; or to give a voice to the suppressed and the vulnerable; or to raise the aspirations of the underprivileged.

The energy that such students (and pleasingly, there are many) bring to tutorials is impressive, and we hate to restrain their purposes and commitment, but often restraint must be exercised in the interests of unbiased research (and a consequent good grade). We often must advise caution, because for the purposes of an assessed research project, it is not advisable to pursue a methodological direction which is founded so overtly on a personal or ideological position, irrespective of your commitment to inclusivity.

Example 1. Pheobe. A Staunch Advocate of EDI

Phoebe was a tremendously impressive, energetic, and impassioned trainee teacher of Computing at a school in Dorset, and she tried indefatigably to be an influencer and a vocal role model for girls everywhere. Phoebe was interested in the proportion of girls opting to take Science, Technology, Engineering and Mathematics (STEM) subjects at 'A' level. She wanted girls to consider STEM subjects as a means to a powerful career. In her school's 'A' level groups when Phoebe was there, girls made up 51% of the chemistry cohort (which pleased her) and 39% of the mathematics cohort (which she felt was not too bad), but Phoebe was so disappointed that in her 'A' level computing classes, girls constituted only 15% of the cohort, and similar figures pertained in previous years. She had read that nationally, amongst computing, engineering and STEM courses at further or higher education, girls comprise fewer than 33% of students, and Phoebe was determined that this should change. Specifically, it should start to change in her secondary school in Dorset.

We can see that Phoebe is motivated by equality and inclusion. In particular, she has a passion for gender equality. When she speaks, Phoebe is quite transparent that her passion for inclusion means inclusion for girls, specifically in STEM subjects. She is not excluding boys, but every day she uses every opportunity to inspire as many girls as possible to aim high, break glass ceilings, and at least consider computing and engineering as career aspirations.

Because Phoebe is so consistently committed to her passion to raise girls' aspirations in this way, she intended to harness her research project to this end too. Her proposed research project title was 'How can more girls be encouraged to choose computing as an 'A' level option in a secondary school in Dorset?', and she wanted to find out the answer to that question by asking the girls about it – the girls who will be making that actual choice. She was proposing to undertake a case study to that effect.

━━━━━━━ **Reflective Questions 8.1** ━━━━━━━

Before you read on, please consider why a tutor might discourage Phoebe from this research project title, in terms of EDI.

We would argue that despite Phoebe's clear and ongoing commitment to gender equality, her research title, and the consequent methodology that she claims it would engender (a case study) are flawed. There appear to be all the trappings of inclusivity and equality here, because Phoebe's commitment to instigate positive change is obvious, but the problem is that she intends her research project to be a means to an end. She is confusing action research with a case study (see Chapter 3). Her proposed title identifies a perceived problem (perceived by Phoebe) that needs solving, but this is not a problem that has been raised by any of the girls prior to Phoebe's recruitment and data collection. This is a problem that will be projected by Phoebe onto the individual girls who will participate in her research project. Rather than neutrally collecting the undirected perceptions, attitudes and stories of her individual participants regarding what factors they consider when choosing 'A' level options, Phoebe is using the project to influence them, even if that influence is just to plant a question amongst them, and even if it is for their own good (at least in Phoebe's view). We know this is Phoebe's aim because Pheobe openly told us this. She is opportunistically using her case study as an instrument of change amongst her school in Dorset. But that is not what a case study is primarily trying to achieve. Case study research should only be undertaken to collect data about an existing phenomenon, not to influence participants or to instigate change. Phoebe might moderate her title to read 'What factors are discouraging girls in a secondary school in Dorset from choosing computing as an 'A' level option?', but even that still suggests that by failing to choose computing in sufficient numbers, the girls are collectively doing something wrong or disappointing, or at best unambitious. Phoebe's laudable commitment to equality and female empowerment has skewed the ethics of her study. We had to suggest to Phoebe that she only researched pupils' existing perceptions and experiences regarding their 'A' level choices and not try to use her study to drive an agenda for change.

You may be interested to learn that Phoebe eventually chose to undertake a literature-based research project, avoiding the requirement to collect data. Her passion was contained in her original proposed title, and she was not interested in watering it down. If she was going to talk to girls about subject choices and career options, it was not part of Phoebe's make up to remain neutral. She wanted to actively inspire and empower, not to passively collect and collate. Instead, Phoebe elected to use national statistics, Ofsted reports, governmental policy statements and supporting documentation along with a wide range of published literature to answer her question. She was highly successful in her project, but her choice of a literature-based study was taken because Phoebe knew that for her, talking with female pupils (or even with other members of staff) was to try to inspire them to become strong women and to push the boundaries of the possible. She wanted to change norms and empower people, not passively study them. Pheobe appreciated that she was not a natural researcher, because neutrality was not in her character. A literature-based study was very much the right (and ethically safe) option for her.

THREE SAFE AND ESSENTIAL WAYS TO PROMOTE INCLUSIVITY IN YOUR RESEARCH PROJECT

So, if a zealous commitment to EDI such as that held by Phoebe is to be discouraged, how might you demonstrate to your marker ways in which you have promoted inclusion within your research project? The following three aspects of inclusion are those we consider to be the most recommended and adopted amongst the many students we have supervised. None of the three fit obviously with a commitment to Equality and Diversity. Rather they seem to us to come under the category of inclusive common sense. We suggest you consider each of them as a minimum for your study, and that you identify your response to them in your methodology, with examples, to demonstrate to your marker your practical commitment to inclusive practice. Weak research projects often fail to take any of these three into consideration at all.

Language Use

You will already be aware of the importance of language use if you are engaging with children of whatever age, and how essential it is to make sure your vocabulary is age appropriate. However, it may come as a surprise to you if you are new to research that you will certainly need to consider this for adults too. Too many research students fail to take this into consideration. You must make sure the vocabulary you use is understood by everyone. All professions use technical language and acronyms. You must ensure that the vocabulary you use is understood by your participants. For example, we know students who have included words and acronyms within their interview or survey questions such as constructivism, metacognition, flipped classroom, individual education plan, education health and care plan, and assessment for learning. These are terms and acronyms that you might expect your participants to know, but therein lies the problem. Students who blithely use such terms with participants when collecting data are basing their chosen vocabulary around their own expectations of things that their participants 'ought' to know and understand. It is probably true that most experienced teachers would know the meaning of each of those terms, and that most inexperienced teachers might, but Learning Support Assistants probably would not. The words 'probably' and 'most' are, by definition, not enough when it comes to inclusion. We would therefore advise you to use non-technical vocabulary in your questions and define acronyms as you go along as a matter of course. Yes, you must allow participants to use whatever vocabulary they want to, but do not risk embarrassing or isolating them by premising your questions around technical jargon that you rather arrogantly think they are bound to understand. This is another reason why a pilot can be so important and revealing (Chapter 7).

Make Sure Your Data Collection Processes Are First and Foremost Based on the Needs of Your Participants, Not on Your Needs

Design your data collection experiences around the needs of your participants. Will children have to miss all or part of their lunch break time to be involved in your study? Would adult participants prefer to talk to you individually rather than in a group? How long will the interviews, tasks, or questionnaires take, and is that time demand reasonable or possible for them? Again, this is why a pilot can be so important.

Additionally. it may well be that you have devised fifteen highly relevant questions around your research title, but if an exploration of all fifteen is likely going to take more time than busy professional participants can or want to give you, what is the point of having fifteen? This leads directly to the third consideration regarding inclusion.

Make Sure Your Data Collection Processes Are First and Foremost Designed to Identify the Views of Your Participants, Not to Confirm Yours

If you have a long list (more than about eight) of very specific and possibly sequential interview questions that you have chosen to ask your participants, this suggests that you have already decided the direction of travel for your interviews, and where the interviews are going to go. In our experience, lots of students claim in their methodology that they are undertaking semi-structured interviews, when that is not really the case. In an effective semi-structured interview, participants will have the opportunity to express whatever attitudes, opinions and perceptions they hold concerning your research area, and there will be flexibility in where the interview goes, within loose parameters. Yes, this can make it harder to analyse the data, because a wide range of views may be expressed by your different participants, but the interview is not about you or your needs. If you are to be inclusive, the interview should not be designed around your preconceptions, preferences or worries about data presentation. It is very easy to analyse data and identify patterns contained within them when you have imposed a stranglehold over what is being talked about (remember Molly in chapter 2). It is harder to analyse a wide spectrum of responses, but if you want to be inclusive, and to allow participants to express the things that are important to them and that they would therefore want to be included (things that you may or may not have thought of prior to the interview), that is what you must enable and encourage.

Further Research Project Examples

Here are further research project examples that explore issues raised in this chapter.

Example 2: William. A Very Good Idea, Poorly Executed

William, training to teach History in a large secondary school in Kent, is not convinced that a written report is the best means of assessing his Year 8's knowledge and understanding of the lessons he has given on the English Civil War. His apprehension comes from an awareness that some of the Year 8 children in his classes lack confidence in their written work and as such he suspects from conversations he has had with them that they know and understand more than they can successfully write. William considers this assessment process to be therefore flawed. For his research project, he decides to ask the research question *'Can non-typical forms of assessment enable Year 8 children in a secondary school in Kent to demonstrate their knowledge and understanding about historical events better than in a traditional written report?'* William teaches three parallel Year 8 classes. He decided to separate them and ask the students in two of the classes to devise a board game in groups of about four. The board game comprises of statements with positive and negative consequences which apply when landing on given squares, perhaps along the lines of Snakes and Ladders or Monopoly. An example statement about the war is 'The power of parliament is strengthened. Have another turn'. William will subsequently ask the children in these classes to write the individual written report they would have ordinarily done in the first place. The other class will do the written report first, and in groups devise the game second. William intended to compare the written reports for content, hoping to see improvement in the written reports by the class that devised the game before doing the written task. If there was time and opportunity William intended to interview three or four students from each of the classes, asking them about these two different assessment activities, what they got out of each, how they found the devising of the game as an assessment tool.

What resulted was much better than William intended. Rather than comparing the written reports of the three classes, he found that it was more illuminating and interesting to compare the content of the written reports with the board games each produced by the same students. In almost all cases the widespread death and destruction engendered by the English Civil War was mentioned prominently in both the game and the written reports, as was the high taxation, famine and the confiscation of land, but the positive aspects of this period (beginnings of religious tolerance, a professional army, the end of the absolute power of the monarchy) featured much more heavily in the board games than in the reports. William was pleased to be able to report differences in perceptions about the impact of the war (for example in one group, Charles I is executed, miss a turn; in another, Charles I is executed, go forward six places). By contrast, William was surprised, and a bit disappointed, that there was no significant difference between the written report work produced by the children depending on which order they did the tasks.

William only had time to interview one group of students about their experiences. Key responses were that the students did not feel patronised by the board game task. They felt they were forced to consider the different positives and negatives much more in the board game than the written report because they had to think of things that happened in the war which would result in rewards and penalties in the board game. They liked working as a group. William was very interested in one student's response about the game that 'Yes, it was good fun, but it's not proper assessment though, is it?'

William's idea was an excellent one for a research project, but he made three mistakes (two of them connected) that reduced his grade. The two connected mistakes were firstly that he gave equal prominence to the data secured from the single group interview with that from the data secured for the work that all the students produced. The way he made analysis of the interviews unintentionally implied that the views held by the four students he spoke with were representative of the whole Year 8 cohort. Since the most compelling data came from the comparisons between the different types of work produced by the children, that should have been the main thrust of his analysis, and the foundation of his conclusions. The interview should have been presented as an interesting aside but acknowledged as unrepresentative since it only involved four students. Secondly, William was so intrigued by the comment that 'it's not proper assessment' that he was sidetracked for some time by it, investing about 500 words of his data analysis in an exploration of that single phrase from a single participant. This extended consideration had no relevance to William's original research question, and so the longer he was off focus, the more his grade fell.

William's third mistake was that although he asked the students and their parents to sign consent forms, not all students returned these forms. William, however, undertook the whole-class activities with all the Year 8s. This does not in itself constitute a big ethical problem (see Chapter 4) as long as a researcher is careful to avoid analysing the data from children who have not opted in. William was not careful. Yes, he only interviewed and analysed the written reports from opted-in students, but his method-ology gave no indication that he had organised the students for the board game activity by grouping together those who had opted in, and those who had not. This was because William had not done that. The opted-in students and those who had not opted-in had all been mixed together in producing the board games, so inevitably the responses and contributions of non-opted-in students had been analysed within each group, as there was no way of knowing who had suggested what. This, from a research point of view, was a big error. William was so busy answering his research question, he lost sight of the need to conduct his research ethically, and to demonstrate how he had done so. William's grade was 55% (there were other problems in his work too, such as inconsistent referencing and grammar problems). He was disappointed generally, but mainly he was annoyed with himself when he realised how easily the ethics problem could have been avoided by careful grouping. A very good and unusual research method had been spoilt by poor attention to ethics.

Example 3: Layan. A Good Idea, Well-Executed in the Main, but Hampered by Being Over-Theorised

Layan, a primary trainee, came to England from Syria, aged 6, and spoke no English when she arrived. Her research project sought to explore how children with English as an Additional Language (EAL) are identified and supported within schools and the extent to which teachers consider the interventions and strategies they use to be effective in supporting children's learning. Earlier in her training, when writing an essay for a module on Inclusion, Layan had been intrigued when she discovered the seminal 1970s work of Jim Cummins and his separation of Basic Interpersonal Communication Skills and Cognitive/Academic Language Proficiency (BICS and CALP). She was amazed when she realised, 15 years after her arrival in England, the extent to which Cummins' theoretical language-development concept reminded her about her own experience of learning and using different aspects of the English language in the developmental stages of her own learning of English. For her research project she interviewed six teachers, five from her final placement school drawn from across Key Stages 1 and 2, and one who taught in a secondary school (a friend).

Layan was careful not to ask any leading questions in the interviews, but she was interested to note that the teachers were less confident when responding to the questions about how their schools identified children with EAL than they were when speaking about strategies. In early parts of the interviews the teachers each spoke eloquently about ways in which they fostered language-rich learning environments, how they separated compositional aspects of writing from transcriptional, how they encouraged children to repeat instructions and to verbalise their thinking, but when asked about how the schools identified children with EAL in the first place, or assessed their continuing but changing needs, responses tended to be no more than saying they had been given a list of names at the start of the academic year. When Layan introduced the concept of BICS and CALP to her participants towards the end of the interviews, the teachers' responses became stilted. Most had not heard of this theory, and Layan realised in hindsight that its introduction to her interviews had been counterproductive. Layan had assumed that the teachers would know about the theory, and would therefore find that it helped them to talk about how difficult or otherwise it is to identify the extent to which each child with EAL needed support, or whether, in the case of the secondary teacher, targeted support needed to continue. She assumed the theory would help the teachers to talk about how it relates to the difficulty of assessing the English language proficiency of such children, for example if the child operates fluently in conversational aspects of English use (BICS: pass the ruler please; what did you have for lunch?; I like your hair) but struggles to articulate technical, curriculum vocabulary, for example of the water cycle (CALP: evaporation, condensation, precipitation, collection). None of this, however, happened in the interviews. Indeed, the bits of the interviews that gave Layan good data were exclusively the bits before she started to talk to the teachers about theory. After that point, the interviews began to disintegrate. Layan realised, too late, that although her knowledge about BICS and CALP was helpful as a theoretical underpinning for her analysis of the data, it made her participant teachers uneasy when she asked them about how their practice was informed by this theoretical concept. Had Layan simply written about Cummins' BICS and CALP in her literature review, and had she then kept it in the back of her mind when she was analysing the responses of the teachers, referring to it in her data analysis if and when one or more of them said things that resonated with it, that would have been a strong thing to do. It is one thing (and a good thing) to have a theoretical position in mind when undertaking a research project. It is quite another to interrogate your participants about their understanding and use of it.

Example 4: Maisie: An Attempt at Mixed Methods, Insensitively Outworked

Maisie, a primary trainee in Key Stage 2 (Year 5), wanted to include two very different forms of data collection because she had heard of mixed methods research, and being an ambitious student, wanted to try it. Simply put, mixed methods are used in studies which collect both quantitative and qualitative data so that different perspectives can apply to the research question. Maisie's question was *'What are Key Stage 2 children's perceptions regarding the portrayal of gender stereotypes in picture books?'* Even though Maisie was hosted in a Year 5 class, she undertook her research with Year 4s, in an overt (and creditable) attempt to demonstrate how she tried to minimise Social Desirability Bias (Chapter 6). Maisie decided to read two picture books, in which the protagonist of each was female, to six groups of four children (two groups of girls, two groups of boys, and two mixed groups) and asked the children about their reactions to these books. The books were 'The Paperbag Princess' (Munsch & Martchenko, 1980) and 'A Dress with Pockets' (Murray & Løvlie, 2022). For her commitment to mixed methods, Maisie also decided to make quantitative analysis of the school's picture book area of the library, counting how many books had mainly male protagonists, how many had female, and how many were neutral.

━━━━ Reflective Questions 8.2 ━━━━

Please stop to consider any potential problems, methodological or ethical, that might arise here if Maisie is not careful (and she wasn't).

The project was very successful in terms of the interview data. Maisie was careful not to project onto the children her strongly held objections to the gender inequality in children's picture books, but instead asked them neutral questions to try to ascertain their own perceptions. She was delighted to discover that most Year 4 children in her study were aware of the term 'stereotype' and were conscious of the gendered nature of these two books. This was true of the boys' and the girls' groups, but pleasingly (for Maisie) the two groups of girls were quite animated about it, whereas the groups of boys were less so, and interestingly, the mixed groups were less animated still. All this fed into Maisie's gender focus perfectly. Three problems, however, arose for Maisie later. The first two she was conscious of before the submission of her project, the third she was not.

The first problem arose when Maisie started to tally the picture books in the school library. For one thing it took much, much longer than she thought it would, and for another, the school librarian (Mrs Blake, a Year 1 teacher) had long been ahead of Maisie in her awareness of gender inequality in the school library, and over the last few years had systematically been stocking the library with books with female protagonists and books in which the genders shared the power. These last books were very difficult for Maisie to categorise, and she got herself a bit confused over the criteria for each category. It is hard to do mixed methods when your counting system is ambiguous. Nonetheless Maisie ploughed on and despite her vague categorisation, eventually felt able to identify that male protagonists were indeed disproportionately over-represented in the school library, which was a finding that sat well with her initial hypothesis. Maisie felt able to declare this even though Mrs Blake had been trying to address the imbalance for some years.

This led to the second problem for Maisie, which was huge, and which she had not seen coming at all. Mrs Blake, who was obviously aware of Maisie's study and was interested in it, was seriously offended. She had been diligently trying to realign the library on a limited budget, and Maisie's thoughtlessness, and rather ambiguously calculated and dismissive analysis of the school library upset her. A lot. To her credit, Maisie realised the error she had made, apologised profusely to Mrs Blake, and immediately promised not to report the library findings, and to destroy all her data about the library. Also, to Maisie's great credit, in her submission she reported what had happened, how she now realised that her tally criteria were insufficiently transparent and granular, and how she had responded to the hurt she had caused. If only Maisie had simply interviewed the children, and perhaps also interviewed Mrs Blake about gender aspects of picture books in the library, all would have been well. After this faux pas, Maisie did not feel able to ask Mrs Blake for an interview.

The third problem arose in Maisie's analysis. Her research question was '*What are Key Stage 2 children's perceptions regarding the portrayal of gender stereotypes in picture books?*'. Maisie, however, with less data to explore than she had originally intended and perhaps still recovering from the library incident, chose to not only analyse the responses that the children made, but she went to some length to report the differences in animation showed by the groups of girls, the groups of boys, and the mixed groups. Maisie's title does not promise a gendered analysis. She speaks only of 'Key Stage 2 children'. In hindsight she would have been better to amend her title to 'Are there differences in boys' and girls' perceptions regarding the portrayal of gender stereotypes in picture books?' This is a nuanced point, and Maisie was not penalised at all heavily for it, but making the title fit the data analysis is an important aspect of a research project. Projects evolve. It is not cheating to make changes to your research title after you have collected your data. Indeed, if interesting and unexpected findings arise, we would recommend revisiting your title from time to time to make sure it remains relevant to interesting and compelling aspects of the data.

Maisie's research project attracted a grade of 68%, not least because of her honesty about her method, and a very strong literature review. She went into the project all evangelical and enthusiastic but emerged at the other end rather bloodied and bruised, but along the way she learnt a lot about research methods, ethics, and keeping people's feelings in mind when planning a project. We reiterate again, and cannot stress this enough, the successful and positive answering of your research question is not the most important thing when conducting a research project. A demonstration of your understanding of the process is as important as the product.

SUMMARY

The main points we hope you have taken from this chapter are:

- If you hold passionate and evangelical views on a subject, you need to consider very carefully whether you can conduct a neutral research project with that focus.

- If you set out to confirm your own pre-existing attitudes, you probably will, but this is unlikely to lead to a strong grade. A research project should be an exploration of a field or question, not a procession towards a predetermined outcome. Please be warned. If nothing in your project comes as a surprise to you, your resultant low grade might.
- Always use plain simple language when you engage with participants, and do not assume their technical or theoretical knowledge.
- As a corollary to this, it is very easy to upset people with your methods if your needs ideas and views are front and centre of your research project, and you unwittingly and insensitively choose to impose them on other people. The discovery and celebration of your participants' views and experiences is so much more important than if you choose to find ways of confirming your own views and preconceptions.

FURTHER READING

Cummins, J. (1980). The cross-lingual dimensions of language proficiency: Implications for bilingual education and the optimal age issue. *TESOL Quarterly* Vol. 14, No. 2, pp. 175–187

In this paper, Cummins argues that for children with EAL, academic/curriculum language develops more slowly than interpersonal or conversational language, and the two can be empirically distinguished. This would explain why children with EAL who have apparently developed good interpersonal and communication skills perform less well than expected on standardised tests and examinations.

REFERENCES

Munsch, R., & Martchenko, M. (1980). *The paper bag princess*. Annick Press.

Murray, L., & Løvlie, J. (2022). *A dress with pockets*. Pan MacMillan.

9
LITERATURE REVIEW

━━━━━━━━━━━ **Chapter Aims** ━━━━━━━━━━━

This chapter will explore the following:

- Is a literature review like an essay?
- What is the review trying to achieve?
- What does a good review look like?
- What are features of ineffective reviews?
- Taking a historical approach.
- Types of literature (academic, professional, governmental, reports, and grey literature).
- Which comes first? How is the Literature Review connected to your research questions?
- How to review literature?
- Reading efficiently.

IS A LITERATURE REVIEW LIKE AN ESSAY?

Writing a literature review, particularly if you are new to it, is not easy. This is because although it appears like an essay in many ways, it is different from an essay in purpose.

It is the same as an essay in that it needs a good structure. You are trying to organise information just as you would in an essay (for example it is common to adopt sub-headings), and there will be a sense of argument, purpose and progress. There will be an introduction, identifying where the literature review is going, what its most important points are, and a summarising conclusion. The demand for academic integrity and clear written English is also the same as in an essay. The way you reference your sources is also identical. The need to avoid plagiarism and academic misconduct is the same. Both an essay and a literature review are exercises in clarity, so you will already be familiar with all these features from your experience of writing in an essay format.

There are four fundamental differences, however, between an essay and a literature review. Firstly, an essay is trying to respond to a given, usually imposed, title or question and in it you are perhaps seeking to be persuasive, at least in the conclusion. In contrast, a literature review seeks primarily to identify what is known about a phenomenon or field, and to set what you consider to be the parameters of that field. There is no attempt at persuasion in a literature review. That may come later in your research project. The aim of a literature review is to present what is known about the field within which your research question sits in a neutral, organised, concise, and clear way. You are not making your own arguments as you might in an essay. You are simply showing your understanding of the field by organising it and identifying its main constituent areas or arguments.

Secondly, in an essay your teacher training institution may encourage you to give examples from your own professional experience to contextualise the points you are making, but there is no place for personal experience in a literature review. In a review, you are reviewing the field, not demonstrating your place within it, or your application of it.

Thirdly, whereas an essay is a stand-alone item, a literature review is one component of something bigger, and it needs to be treated as such. Along with your methodology, it is the foundation of your research project. As such, the literature review is not the only aspect of the submission that you are relying upon to attract the grades you are hoping for. In an essay, the literature is all you have got in your quest to answer or respond to the title (along with perhaps examples from your own experience, mentioned above).

This leads to the fourth difference, and this is very important. Your literature review will provide the background, context, or landscape against which you will analyse the data you collect. An essay does not have to deliver this important secondary function, and this is the reason why you must not attempt persuasion in your literature review. When you come to analyse your data, you will be able to identify the extent to which your data resonates with what is known about the field, as clearly identified in your literature review.

But do not worry. If the data or responses you collect do not resonate well with your literature, that is not problematic (Chapter 10 – data analysis). They do not have to. The extent to which they resonate with your literature (or not) are your findings, and you simply present these findings with reference to your literature. Your findings do not have to marry closely to your literature review, and you do not have to make them fit either (indeed, trying to do so would be an error). A strongly structured neutral literature review will make the analysis of your data a much easier task than a weak, opinionated, imprecise one.

So, you are not trying to answer your research question in a literature review as you would in an essay. Instead, you are demonstrating your understanding of the breadth of relevant literature that applies within the field of your chosen research question. Your literature review (along with your methodology) is fundamental to you getting a good grade for your research project, because unlike your data collection chapter, you have full control. You have chosen your literature review's focus and its parameters. You have done the reading in order to discover and identify the compelling aspects of your chosen focus within published work. If you do this well it will contribute favourably to your overall grade. Even if the data you collect for your analysis chapter is disappointing, a strong literature review will go some way to ensuring that you still get the overall grade you deserve for your research project.

WHAT IS YOUR LITERATURE REVIEW TRYING TO ACHIEVE?

First and foremost, in your literature review you are trying to demonstrate your understanding of the field in which your research question sits. You do this by taking your readers by the hand and identifying to them what the most important or compelling arguments, themes or standpoints are in that field. If there are particularly influential writers or documents within the field (for example a government document that is instrumental in setting policy, or a particular writer who is an influential advocate or critic of that policy), you will identify who and what they are, why they are important, and the nature and extent of their impact. Your literature review is simply a vehicle for showing your ability to organise your thoughts around the reading you have done.

The words 'you' or 'your' have appeared 86 times in this chapter so far. The literature review needs to act as a vehicle for you to clearly demonstrate your understanding of the literature surrounding the research question or focus you have chosen. But the review must not be treated as a vehicle for your preconceptions or opinions. Absolutely not. The review is not about you or your experiences. The opposite is true. You should be trying to show your tight organisation and clear categorisation of the most relevant sources, together with an ability to filter out aspects that are less compelling or irrelevant. No opinions. No self. Just a neutral analysis of the literature, thus demonstrating your understanding of it.

A strong literature review will be structured around the main themes, and you may choose to use subheadings in order to make crystal clear to your marker what the themes are. We are often asked 'How many themes should there be?' to which the rather unhelpful answer is 'As many as the literature presents', but typically in successful literature reviews that we have assessed there are between three and six. Identifying fewer than three suggests a lack of nuance and granularity. Having more than six suggests a lack of filtering. If there are more than six, you should ask yourself whether all themes are equally compelling. If not, leave the less compelling ones out. This filtering is essential to the production of a strong literature review. If you have the capability to recognise significant arguments from less important ones, and to explain why you consider this to be the case, you are a long way towards achieving that most coveted of academic attributes – critical analysis.

You have heard the phrase 'critical analysis'. You know it is important, but you may still be wondering what this mythical creature looks like, and how you will know if you have met it. Simply put, to analyse is to organise (the clear identification of the most important arguments, points, or themes). To be critical is to explain why they are important; to give them context; or to understand their impact. To be critical is not to criticise. The word comes from the Greek κριτικός ('judgement'), and the Latin criticus (judge). To be critical is to explain, to explore, to assess, and to contextualise. Anyone armed with a computer, an internet connection, and a database can find articles that are relevant to a chosen field or research question. It is really easy to then just list who has said what and call it a literature review. It is much harder to take that raw material and turn it into a satisfying organised, filtered exploration of the field as a whole, but that is where the high grades come from.

■■■■■■■■ **Activity 9.1** ■■■■■■■■

Once you have identified what the main themes are in the field that you have chosen, and when you have completed writing about each of them, we advise you to search for the word 'because' in what you have written. If it does not appear, it is unlikely that you have exercised much in the way of criticality. Why do writers agree or disagree about the importance of this aspect of the field you have chosen? Who are the outliers? Why is this theme important, and who to?

Sentences such as *"This argument/viewpoint/document/policy is essential to an understanding of this subject because ..."* should appear more than once in your literature review, with an explanation that lasts beyond that one sentence.

The word 'because' forces you to be analytical, and so it is your friend in academic writing. If you struggle to complete a sentence after writing 'because ...', then this is a clear indicator that there is something wrong, lacking or weak in your argument or reasoning.

A weak literature review will be an untidy throwing together of names and quotes that you have found concerning things that you consider to be relevant to your research question. Your reader is left to try, on your behalf, to make sense of how they all fit together, and what the most important arguments are. Often in a weak review every sentence starts or finishes with a name. Thomson and Hall (2023) say this. McCleod (2023) considers that. Ozgood (2007) found the other. Shah (2021) reports. Watts (2005) likens. The writing goes on and on like this for paragraphs and pages. The writers of this book have assessed reviews written in this style, and students have experienced resultant disappointment in their grade.

For example, Melissa submitted such a review, and her response to her marker was "But I worked so hard on it. I read so much, and everything I read is in there. I found so many articles and I have left nothing out. All the things I have included show how much I have read".

But therein lies the problem. Melissa left nothing out. Neither did she effectively organise it. Melissa is a serial lister of quotes and sources. Everything she read around her subject was separately squeezed into her literature review, in a way that suggested that all sources and all arguments were equally important and equally valid, seemingly in whatever order she chose to present them. All the ingredients for a satisfying review were there, but Melissa applied no filter or explanation; there was little demonstration or connection between sources which either agreed with each other, connected with each other, or had similar impacts on schools, teachers and/or pupils. There was little in the way of organisation of clear arguments or themes. Through the interminable listing of who has said what, Melissa's literature review was no more than a demonstration of her ability to find relevant sources and bundle them together, and consequently it was not a clear demonstration of her understanding of how the sources cohere into that nebulous thing we call 'the field', even though it was true that she had worked hard on it.

But this was doubly bad news for Melissa, because (unlike an essay) a literature review is not a stand-alone item. It also has to support an analysis of her data. As a direct result of the lack of clarity and coherence in Melissa's literature review, it was all but useless to her when she came to analyse her data against it. How was she to identify the extent to which the data she collected from interviewing teachers (about their classroom management and use of resources in art-based activities) resonated with significant arguments within the field? By presenting an incoherent literature review, she had nothing solid to apply to her data. Her weak literature review failed to help her in her analysis chapter. A weak literature review is a lose-lose situation in a research project.

Melissa's friend Stuart used to be a serial lister but has recognised from feedback that if his grades are to improve, he must change this aspect of his academic writing. He is still not very advanced along his road to improvement, however, because now his strategy is to create a literature review which is, in effect, an "annotated bibliography" (Hart, 2018: 2). In this approach, Stuart searches for sources he considers to be useful and relevant (perhaps particular journal articles, books or government publications), and from those he chooses the ones that he feels most positively speak to his research question. By doing this, he is not overwhelmed by lots of different people or sources saying the same or different things. For his literature review he has chosen five 'good' sources. He then structures his literature review by exploring separately each of the five in turn, identifying the content, and arguments of each, and then, one by one, applying each to his research question, being careful to use the word 'because' on each occasion. He was particularly pleased with his sentence that began "An understanding of the Rapid Evidence Review on Pupil Attendance (EEF 2022) is essential to an understanding of this subject because . . .".

Stuart's approach has the benefit of at least giving the review a clear structure and gives Stuart something concrete to use as a backdrop to his research question and to his data analysis. There is also some explanation in his review, which he knows is essential. But the weakness of this strategy of course is that it is a very compartmentalised approach which gives the impression that the chosen sources represent (or at least speak to) the entirety of the field, which may or may not be true. Whereas Mellisa found so many sources with something to say that she struggled to organise them, Stuart discounted all but five good ones. This approach suggests to his marker that Stuart has only read five sources to any depth and that he has therefore reviewed only a very small part of the literature, chosen by the sources' relevance to his preconception of the answer to his question. His markers will not be able to award the grades Stuart is hoping for because of such a narrow approach.

Taking a Historical Approach

Sometimes a historical approach can be helpful, but do be careful. If your research question sits within an area of regular policy innovation (for example early reading, children's mental health, safeguarding) then a brief overview of how we came to be where we are, policy-wise, can be a useful tool for contextualising your arguments or presenting what within the field is influential. You must be careful, however, not to just present a list. First this thing happened, and then this policy was announced, then we had a change of government, then there was Covid, followed by the publication of that white paper which heralded the announcement of a new policy, and this impacted a new Ofsted inspection framework (. . . continues for three paragraphs). If it is essential to identify all these things, then do so, but if you do no more than simply list what happened and when, this is no better than Melissa's serial listing of sources. You must say why you are including this information, for example by writing, 'An *awareness of the historical context is essential to an understanding of this subject because* . . .'. If you cannot compellingly finish that sentence, do not waste valuable wordcount on an inessential aside, which will read to your marker as waffle and unnecessary padding.

TYPES OF LITERATURE

When you search for literature using a library search or a database such as Elton Bryson Stevens Company (EBSCO), you may wonder what the various types of literature are, and whether they are useful to you. The most common type of result by far will be academic journal articles, but you are also likely to be presented with some books, eBooks, doctoral dissertations and periodicals.

The first three of these are to be wholeheartedly recommended to support your literature review. Each is peer reviewed and so carries academic integrity. As well as the contents themselves, the bibliographies contained in journal articles are good indicators of influential sources. If many of the articles cite the same sources or authors, this is a good indicator that those sources or authors are influential within the field.

Dissertations tend to be doctoral theses. These are also useful for their bibliographies, but dissertations tend to be very much bigger than journal articles and so will be time consuming for you to engage with.

Periodicals include such things as professional journals. Articles found within periodicals tend to be written by practitioners such as teachers or associated professionals, and usually have a practical focus. The articles go through at least an editorial process, and many, not all, are peer reviewed. They are interesting and will be relevant to your research question, but do not carry the same weight as an academic journal. For this reason, you can cite periodicals, but do not base a whole argument on them.

You might also cite *grey literature*. Grey literature comprises of publications which are not peer reviewed but are extremely influential within the field. Examples of these are government policy documents, white papers, ministerial speeches and announcements, Ofsted reports, and conference papers.

During the Covid crisis grey literature also included blogs. This was because researchers, especially medical researchers, wanted to get their research published extremely quickly. Since then, some academics continue to publish using blogs. We do not recommend you cite blogs unless you are absolutely certain that the author or publisher is extremely reputable. The future of the blog as a publishing tool within academic circles remains contested, and so for the purposes of your research project, we recommend you stay within the parameters of journals and books.

Do not cite newspapers at all, unless you are using them as an example or indicator of media perception.

You should also avoid citing websites in a generic way. If you do find information on a website, try to discover and identify the source. It is much better to cite a specific document, for example the National Curriculum (DfE 2013), than the generic www.gov.co.uk website you may have found it on which is far too imprecise a citation.

WHICH COMES FIRST? HOW IS THE LITERATURE REVIEW CONNECTED TO YOUR RESEARCH QUESTION?

There should be a degree of equality between your research question and your literature review, so that neither is allowed to dictate what the other will contain or look like. For example, it is a weak and dangerous thing to decide upon your research question and then simply set about finding articles that are relevant to it, because there is a danger that you will only search for sources or arguments that support your preconception of the probable answer to your question, and you may consciously or unconsciously omit to engage with literature that you thoughtlessly deem irrelevant or unhelpful. Hempel (2020) identifies two types of bias when developing a literature review: *selection bias* (often an unconscious bias where you seek and explore only those themes which fit with your preconception, for example through a narrow choice of keywords in your initial searches); and *reporting bias* (in which you report only those things which fit your preconception). This is usually consciously done, certainly by weaker students who are not sure what to do with multiple positions or conflicting arguments. In this scenario, the research question is overtly driving the content and parameters of the literature review, especially if you are guilty of both of those biases, which is easily done if you are not careful.

By contrast, Femi is interested in exploring the experiences of male teachers in Key Stage 1, working as they do in a predominantly female environment. Femi has heard about selection bias and is keen to demonstrate to his supervisor and markers how he wants nothing to do with it. A search in Google Scholar using only the phrase 'Male teachers in Key Stage 1' and no other key words resulted in 3.8 million results (17,700 when the date range was customised to the last ten years) and the search returned articles on male teachers' identity; sexuality; the 'feminised curriculum'; male teachers in Ireland (and Australia, and Dubai); teaching manfully; children's perceptions of male teachers (myth-busting the 'dad effect'); gendered role modelling; the 'boy problem'; the (de)construction of heterosexual masculinity; teaching emotional intelligence; gender bias in STEM subjects – the list continues. Femi is completely overwhelmed. By contrast the same phrase in EBCSO resulted in just two results, both of them the same (about the ambiguities of re-gendering the Key Stage 1 environment, which is not Femi's passion at all). In a tutorial, his supervisor suggests he looks at only the titles of the first 20 or 50 results that Google Scholar has presented, and from these he should select between three and five sources that seem most aligned to the initial vision he had for his project. As well as reading those few sources, the supervisor suggests that Femi should then explore their bibliographies to find other sources which will be relevant to his focus. In this way the literature will inform (but not dictate) what Femi's final research project title is likely to be. His title may yet evolve as Femi reads beyond those sources. Any commonalities found within the expanding number of sources will also serve to identify to Femi who the more influential sources or authors are likely to be within the field, and he can then interrogate those sources still further. Still, the title may change as he goes along. Femi is thus building some flexibility regarding his title through his literature review search method. His final title will be informed by, but not dictated by, his literature search.

READING EFFICIENTLY

Inexperienced researchers and many higher education students tend to be very inefficient readers. Agatha was a very inefficient reader. She could spend hours wading through articles, book chapters and government publications, and at the end of all that time she was none the wiser about her subject apart from a few quotes and statistics that she had saved to use later. Agatha acknowledged that she was a passive reader. She lacked goals when she was reading. For example, when she found academic sources, she would then read them unquestioningly from beginning to end. Often, she did not really understand the content or the relevance of what she was reading to her research question, particularly when she was reading the methodology or data analysis sections of journal articles. When she did understand it, she accepted without question what she was reading, since if it had been published, it must be true. When asked what strategies she used to read sources, Agatha looked confused and answered "Well, I just read them. Doesn't everybody?".

Well, no. Not everybody does that. Indeed, we recommend you do not. Here we list some strategies that we recommend you employ. Some we are sure you do already, but we list them here to allay any fears that you (and Agatha) may have that these strategies might be either short-cuts or cheating. They are neither of those things. Rather, they are positive strategies which will save you a great deal of time and thus enable you to engage more widely in literature.

Have a Goal (Usually Singular) When You Are Reading

Become an active reader. Make sure there is a product in what you read, or some planned identifiable movement in your understanding or readiness to write about what you have read. A key feature of efficient reading is that what you read and how you read it is always planned. Your goal may be that you want to identify a selection of sources that you will read; or that you want to answer a question; or to explore a field; to explore an argument within that field; to compare what appear to be two conflicting or similar arguments; to compare and understand particular vocabulary; to explore an author; to identify the chronology or impact of a policy; to identify which arguments or writers are most compelling or influential in a field; to consider the application of a particular theoretical position on professional practice; to identify the extent to which an argument or position is contested. That is a long menu from which you should choose one at a time. Agatha's passivity in reading was actually laziness on her part for two reasons. Firstly, she was unconsciously expecting the author to do all the work. She let the literature wash over her, hoping some would stick. Secondly, she randomly grazed on the literature, assuming that one source would be representative of all the rest. She thought this because she had not learnt to interrogate what she was reading in any way. Agatha had never read any academic source that made her angry, or that she knew she agreed with strongly. Her passivity meant that she was often bored when reading, and because Agatha had no goals, she was never motivated or rewarded by success.

Skim and Scan Read First

To avoid allowing our students (including Agatha) to be passive readers, an exercise we ask them to do is as follows. We give them ten minutes to identify the main points and most compelling sources contained in a previously unseen article. As part of the task, they are required to say specifically how many main points there are. As such, they do not have time to read the article from beginning to end, or even to read it at a comfortable leisurely pace. They have to get a move on. If they are to be successful in this particular task, they have to skip the methodology section and the data analysis. Rather, the students discover to their joy and relief that they only have time to read the abstract, the introduction and the conclusion. They are looking for specifics. They also discover that the ten minutes is passed in frenetic and high-energy activity. It would not be possible for them to sustain that level of concentration for very long. After engaging students with this activity, we are always interested when some students identify perhaps three main points, while others may list five. The students' discussion that follows is then about why many or few of them consider some arguments to be more compelling than others. Initially unbeknown to the students, what they are doing is filtering literature, interrogating it, and identifying the extent to which it is relevant or irrelevant to a research question. Their reading is intensive in energy and concentration, and as a result it is highly time efficient.

Make Your Reading Timebound

As a corollary to the above suggestion, we recommend you give yourself ambitious time restrictions for your reading, at least from time to time. Depending on the goal you choose, sometimes it will be ambitious to achieve something in one or two hours. Sometimes it will be in ten or twenty minutes. It will very rarely be in four hours, because if you are an active reader, four hours is a long time to concentrate that hard.

You might already be someone who ringfences time in the library or at home. Before undertaking the activity described above, Agatha used to often ringfence four hours at a time reading, because she could and felt that she should. Although she was a diligent and hard-working student and she always committed huge amounts of time to her studies, she now realises that she was a very lazy reader. She did not work hard at her reading at all, because she did not know how to. Now she tells herself 'By 11am I will have found the main points in that article' (or compared the views of these two authors; or identified areas of similarity across these six sources; or 'properly' read an article she previously scanned; or will understand these words or vocabulary: or will have written a 500-word synopsis of the main arguments). Now, if she is feeling very confident, Agatha might make sure there is something else in her diary at 11am to make sure she is faithful to her ambition (but this is advanced time-ringfencing, which Agatha is not yet consistently confident to do, but she promises herself she will, one day).

Have a Variety of Reading Styles in Your Repertoire

Agatha's problem was that she knew only one way to read academic texts. Were you to search for 'Active Reading Types' in Google or through AI, you would be confronted with a variety of different lists or analyses, ranging from elementary phonics strategies to organised reading taxonomies. Our experience with research project students, however, suggests the following four strategies are very useful. In the main, they are best seen as sequential, but you do need all of them. Students who only do stages a-c rarely demonstrate much in the way of understanding. Students who miss stages a-c rarely demonstrate sufficient breadth of reading. Although each is very different from the others, as a suite of approaches, employed as a team, they form a very effective approach to academic reading.

Skim Reading

This allows you to decide whether a text is likely to be relevant, and therefore whether or not to give the source more attention later. In a journal article this might only involve the exploration of the abstract and keywords. In a book chapter you might not look beyond headings or subtitles. Be careful though. Have broad inclusion categories. Don't reject more texts than you accept at this stage.

Scan Reading

This is the exercise described in the student task above. In scan reading, you know through your skim reading what you are looking for and what you expect to find, and you are now seeking to identify, categorise or list aspects of the source or sources. Scan reading is more specific than skim reading because you will have a specific product (perhaps a list of main points) or a greater sense of direction at the end of it. Remember to scan the bibliographies as well as the texts to try to identify commonalities in bibliography entries. Who is being cited by lots of people? Promise yourself to find out why.

Categorisation Reading

Here you are looking for patterns within the literature you have scanned, connections between sources, and relevance to your research question and themes. It may be that during this stage your research question starts to evolve through your organisation or categorisation of the sources you have found. Perhaps you will have discovered some surprises, or areas of the field that you have not previously considered, and your intended title may start to change as a result. This is a good thing if it happens, because it shows your thinking is developing and broadening. You are still in the 'getting your-head-around-the-subject stage' here, but by now you are already quite advanced in your thinking about the subject, even though you have yet to read many sources 'properly'. Your categorisation reading will lay the foundation for the structure of your written literature review. What are the most common themes or arguments? Promise yourself to explore each more thoroughly in the 'Reading for Retention' stage.

Retention Reading

Here you are looking to gain a deeper understanding of the subject. This is where you start to read 'properly', taking in the nuances of what you are reading, and considering which arguments you find most compelling, and why. Prior to this (stages a-c) you have been seeking the content and structure of your literature review. Now you are reading texts for understanding. Any ambitious time constraints which you imposed on yourself in the earlier stages of your reading may have to be more generous or flexible here. Knowledge is easily discovered, whereas understanding takes a bit more time. It may help if you have other students with similar interests to talk to and compare your understanding with theirs.

Retention reading used to be Agatha's starting position, which is why it took her so much time and resulted in so little reward. It made her reading very inefficient. Ironically, starting at this fourth stage, as she used to, meant that she did not retain much, because she had not put in the spadework prior to reading for retention. This is why her reading felt so laborious and directionless, and why she was often bored.

HOW TO REVIEW LITERATURE

Having read around your subject, and gained a degree of insight about it, you must now actually write it. One of the most surprising things about an understanding of the processes involved in reviewing literature is the realisation that a literature review is not only about the literature. It is also very much about your understanding of it, and the attitudes you hold towards the writers in the field. If you see the published sources as a means to an end; as a resource to be mined and used as you see fit for your own research project purposes, then your literature review is likely to be quite poor. In this scenario, you are likely to view the literature as a series of individual publications to be accepted or rejected according to your own pre-existing preferences and criteria. As a result, the most important filter in this situation is you, and as a result the literature review would not be driven by the literature, but by your intentions for how the literature is to be used. The scenario shows that if you are being selective about what to report, the main arguments could be predetermined by you even before you start.

Imagine this ridiculous scenario as an analogy. You are in a supermarket looking for ingredients for a meal with friends this evening – perhaps for stuffed avocados. That feta cheese looks nice, you think, so you take plenty of that. That parsley and those tomatoes look appealing, so they go in your trolley. Since you have no experience of getting the stone out of avocados, however, and a friend once told you it is a bit dangerous and more trouble than it is worth anyway, you decide to ignore that bit of the recipe, and so you leave the avocados on the shelf. Your selection of ingredients has been skewed by your own preformed negative attitudes towards avocados. That evening, you serve stuffed avocado to your friends, but without any avocado.

Similarly, a literature review is not a vehicle for answering your research question even before you have collected any data. It is not a recipe, the parameters of which will result in a predetermined product. An example of very weak practice would be if you were to decide what the key features of your research question are (based presumably on your own preconceptions and experience of the field) and then to look exclusively for literature that supports those views. You would then go on to write an extended justification of those views which may or may not be examples of consensus within the field. Therein lies the path to a poor grade, not only because such an approach constitutes overt bias on your part, but it will also have repercussions when you come to formulate the questions you ask if you decide to undertake interviews, questionnaires or surveys. Such deliberately unchallenged preconceptions that you might bring to your selection of literature would inevitably find their way into your research design via the aspects of the field that you choose to ask your participants to explore, share or comment upon.

By contrast, rather than treating the literature as a smorgasbord of disparate resources, if instead you viewed it as a means of discovery; as an opportunity for you to broaden your horizons about an area that interests you greatly; as a process; as a field around which you are trying to develop mastery, then this would be a strong approach, and would pay you dividends, both for your literature review, and in the way this approach informs your research design. If you can develop the capacity to think about the field in broad terms and so can demonstrate that you are starting to develop the ability to make connections between similar viewpoints or perhaps even to identify differences between them, then your review will be strong, and your markers will be impressed.

So, when reviewing literature, you should be drawn towards surprises. Rather than discounting sources that offer views which are counter to your own expectations, or unhelpful to your research question, you should embrace them (and if necessary, let the research question evolve). Those 'I-hadn't-thought-of-that' moments are so important, and you should grab hold of them. We have supported several students who have claimed that there is very little research in their chosen area, and who, after sometimes the most lightweight of interrogation about their statement, have acknowledged that what they mean is there is little literature to support their anticipated findings. Wouldn't it be awful if you failed to identify important understandings, arguments or theoretical positions that are shared by most writers in the field simply because those positions did not fit with your own initial preconceptions?

Imagine you are at a conference listening to a panel discussion about using artificial intelligence (AI) in preparing, writing, and editing assignments. There are seven speakers on the stage, and you have been tasked with reporting to three fellow students (who have each gone to other panel discussions) what the key aspects of the discussion were. In the discussion it was not the case that each of the seven speakers had a certain amount of time to say what they think and then defer to another speaker. They did not speak sequentially. That is not how discussions work, and that format would be very boring to listen to. No. The panel discussion is a conversation in which all seven speakers severally contribute as the focus moves from one theme to another.

When you come to report back to your fellow students, and they report to you, the most important thing they will want to know is what the main points of the panel discussion were. What was covered? What were the most compelling arguments? What are the main implications of using AI for preparing, writing and editing assignments? Yes, your fellow students will be interested to know who articulated the arguments most compellingly, and who was unconvincing or looked a bit out of their depth, but what they most want from you is to have a clear overview of the most important arguments. What things were the seven speakers most interested in conveying to the conference? That is what your fellow students require of you, and this is what your literature review should be like. What are the headlines? Why are these headlines important, and to whom?

Where this analogy breaks down of course is that in your literature review you must indicate (using citations) who holds which view, but still, you will not report who said what in an individual sequential way. Your literature review should not just be a list of who says what. Think of your review as a report on that panel discussion which focused on your area of interest, but with constant indicators from you of which people (plural or singular) contributed to which argument.

SUMMARY

The big messages we hope you take from this chapter are as follows:

- Your literature review is not an essay. It is more than that. An essay is usually an attempt to answer a given question. By contrast, although a literature review firstly identifies the major aspects of a field and demonstrates your understanding of a breadth of relevant literature, it does not initially seek to answer a specific research question. You will need to save that for your data analysis. Unlike an essay, your literature review needs to fulfil a second function, supporting the analysis of the data you collect, which is not required of an essay.

- A literature review can and should draw on a range of source types that we have identified. Academic journals are likely to be the most common. Grey literature is also a welcome strong addition if the publications are relevant, as they help to contextualise theoretical positions.
- It is perfectly acceptable (indeed we encourage it) for you to skim read and scan read sources in the early stages of your literature collection. Reading efficiently is an important academic and research skill. It is not cheating, but you need to employ range of reading strategies to become an effective researcher.
- We have explored how to go about reviewing the literature, noting that your positionality is likely to impact the review, and this impact can be positive or negative, so you need to be conscious of it. You should not see the literature review as a product to be produced, but as a process to be explored and reported on. If you find no surprises in your literature, we suggest that your reading is too narrow or overly prescribed.

FURTHER READING

Hart, C. (2018). *Doing a literature review: Releasing the research imagination* (2nd Edition) London: SAGE.

This book's intended audience is for all research practitioners at different stages of their research career. Research students and accomplished research practitioners are catered for in the simple to complex narrative.

REFERENCES

DfE. (2013). *The national curriculum in England. Framework document for key stages 1 to 4.* Crown Copyright.

Education Endowment Foundation. (2022). *Attendance Interventions, Rapid Evidence Assessment*, London: EEF.

Hempel, S. (2020). *Conducting your literature review.* American Psychological Association. http://www.jstor.org/stable/j.ctv1chs70n

10

DATA ANALYSIS

━━━━━━━━━━ **Chapter Aims** ━━━━━━━━━━

This chapter will explore:

- Different types of approaches to data analysis. Presenting and discussing findings.
- Planning how the data might be presented before collecting it.
- Tables and figures.
- The numbering of tables and figures.
- Five things to avoid in data analysis:
  - 1, Reporting and analysing things that are not found in interview data.
  - 2, Over- and under-interrogation of the data.
  - 3, Seeking and reporting only the data that confirm your preconceptions.
  - 4, Misuse of graphs.
  - 5, Describing graphs and charts.

INTRODUCTION

Whereas you will certainly have written essays prior to undertaking your research project, and this experience will have given you an idea of the academic and structural aspects of writing a literature review, it is perhaps likely that you have never written a data analysis chapter, and so this is all new to you. Most students we support are more uncertain about the data analysis chapter than any other, so if you are feeling apprehensive, you are not alone. There are two aspects of writing a data analysis chapter that are rather different from writing an essay. The first is the structure, and the second is the way in which you give your work academic support. We will explore each in turn.

DIFFERENT TYPES OF APPROACH TO DATA ANALYSIS

The structure of data analysis chapters in published work tends to fall into one of two camps, and the decision about which to adopt is to some extent dependent upon the nature of the data that has been collected. The first approach is to separate the data completely from the discussion and analysis, presenting first one, then the other. For example, if the data is predominantly quantitative, being the result of measuring, counting, tallying and quantifying, this can be an attractive option for researchers. In this approach, the data will simply be set down, usually in charts, graphs, lists, tables, diagrams, scatterplots, histograms or all manner of other mathematical presentation tools. At first, there will be no attempt at explanation or narrative, simply a stark presentation of the raw anonymised data, organised in a way that the reader will be able to easily engage with and navigate, should they wish to. Here, the nature of the selected charts, tables or graphs are designed for two purposes: firstly so that any patterns appearing in the data (or the lack of patterns) are easily and clearly identifiable; and secondly to enable the reader to make a judgement about the extent to which the subsequent data analysis is fair and transparent, again should they wish to (this is an essential characteristic if the writers are hoping to publish in influential academic journals).

Having set down the data in a clear and accessible way, the writer will then go on to make analysis of it (usually termed 'The Discussion section'), where significant aspects of the data are then explored, interrogated and explained. Here, the researcher not only identifies the patterns found within the data, but they will usually also consider the extent to which the data resonates with what is known about the subject (as previously presented in their literature review). As a result, in this part of the writing there will be what is known as a 'dialogue' between the data analysis and the literature review, in that the discussion section is a tightly organised and analytical narrative about what patterns are to be found in the data, and the extent to which they (the data) confirm or challenge existing findings in the field. There will be regular citations to the sources contained in the literature review. Common phrases in the discussion might be 'This pattern in the data supports Parker (2021) and Black (2019), whose results showed similar outcomes' or 'These gender differences do not resonate well with McDonald (2023) whose findings …'. You will recognise the writing style here, which looks very much like essays you have written, but here the citations are not being used to make an argument in themselves, as you may have done in your essays. Rather, they are being used exclusively to give a backdrop, authority and criticality to the data that has been collected in the author's study. It does not matter whether the data does or does not mirror other studies. All the researcher is trying to do is to faithfully demonstrate the extent to which their data fits with those of previous studies. If it does or does not, that is their finding. It is not a weakness if it does not, or a strength if it does.

This first approach of separating the data from the discussion has implications for the reader. Certainly, it is a very solid and transparent approach, but it requires the interested reader to look in two places at once, perhaps flicking backwards and forwards between the discussion and the presentation of data. It also absolves the researcher from the need to apply any filter to the data, at least at first, so every scrap of data can be included and represented. Of course, in quantitative research this is as it should be because effect sizes and statistical significance are dependent on the full range of responses, and it would be a weak thing to do to pick and choose which individual pieces of data should be included and which could be left out. Filters should not be applied to quantitative data unless and until the researcher wants to explore participant subsets (for example, by gender, age or ethnicity or possibly to different stages of the data collection, or different focuses within the study). Researchers adopting quantitative approaches are not looking to identify themes, as qualitative researchers might. Indeed, they are trying to avoid imposing themselves on the data in any way. Rather they are looking for mathematical or statistical patterns and evidence, and the separation of the data from the discussion helps them to concentrate on making their arguments without having to synchronously refer to the details of specific numbers and symbols.

So, the decision to separate the presentation of data from the discussion can work well for research which has generated predominantly quantitative data. But a second approach, in which the presentation of the data is integral to its analysis, can work well if your data are predominantly of a qualitative nature, which is common in social science research projects. There is a skill to this, but most student researchers get better at it in the doing of it.

First and foremost, in this second approach, you must remember that your data analysis chapter is a report. It is not an example of creative writing. It is not an essay. There is no need to manipulate data or fabricate anything to make it fit with something else. Whereas the quantitative researcher can simply present charts and graphs to encapsulate the full extent of their data, the qualitative researcher cannot do that so easily. For example, it is not possible for the qualitative researcher to just list in a table what every participant said. That would take up thousands of words and would also be impossible for the reader to navigate. It would also be very boring. No. The quantitative researcher must apply a filter to the data to make it accessible. The skill is to make sense of the data without seeking to use it to confirm your own expectations. Thinking of it as a report will help you in this. There is a detachment in writing a report which is good practice in data analysis. The writing will feel different from essays you have written, in which you are trying to demonstrate your understanding in response to a question. But you will have already done that in your literature review. There is no need to do it again. In data analysis you are looking to identify the headlines from the data you have collected, and to honestly show the extent to which those headlines cohere and resonate (or not) with the literature you presented.

Laura teaches History at General Certificate of Secondary Education (GCSE), and History and Latin at A Level at an academy in Yorkshire, and she is interested in students' perceptions of whether History is seen as one of the harder or easier subjects at GCSE, and whether this may impact student's GCSE choices. She has interviewed five sixth form students (who did their GCSEs last year); and fifteen students in Key Stage 4 (who are currently taking a History GCSE course) about their perceptions of which GCSE subjects have exams that they consider to be the most difficult. Laura also gave questionnaires to Year 9 pupils who are soon to choose their GCSE options. Having collected all that data, even before Laura wrote a single word of analysis, it was necessary for her to immerse herself in the data to make sense of it. That is not to say that Laura was looking to find where most or fewest pupils agreed with each other, but rather, she was looking to identify what sort of things they most commonly talked about, even if they do or do not agree with each other. Put differently, she was not at first looking for areas where there was a lot of agreement, but rather she was looking within the data for the variety of significant things they talked about. These will become her themes, and once she has those, she can identify (also from the data) the extent to which they offered similar or differing views about them.

To her surprise, Laura found that her participants did agree that science subjects tended to hold a different degree of difficulty than subjects in the humanities or the arts, but she was interested to find that across the participants, and for all three age groups, there was a distinct variety of views about what constitutes difficulty. Several participants thought biology was 'obviously' harder than religious education because biology contained many long technical words and hundreds of facts to learn about how bodies work. But equally, other pupils were adamant that religious education was much harder than biology because pupils had to learn about things which were outside of their own culture or experience and might even challenge their own beliefs. Music was for musicians and therefore very hard if you were not a musician, but easy if you were, because musicians already had a head start. This was considered by most to be fair. Art was not as hard as physics, for the same reason. Also, in art, music, PE, and mathematics there were opportunities to 'do' or demonstrate 'actual skill' in the GCSE assessment of the subject, whereas that was not possible for the student of history, and so history students considered this made it a harder subject to be examined in. There was some degree of consensus that languages, including English, were the hardest subjects of all, but Laura intends to break down the responses to differentiate between the responses of pupils who had English as their first language, and those who did not.

Laura was also surprised that there was little consensus about criteria that might be applied when pupils select their GCSE options. For many, it was about personal interest; for others, it was all about who the teachers were; others wanted to first know what subjects their friends were choosing; and others responded to parental pressure. Some had a career or 'A' level options in mind even when choosing GCSEs.

Laura highlighted four, maybe five, main themes in her data analysis section. At the start of her study, she had only really anticipated the first one. The other three were exclusively informed by her consideration of the data she had collected.

- What are the hardest GCSE exams to be successful in?
- What makes a subject hard?
- What makes the way the subject is examined hard?
- What informs GCSE choices?
- What subjects can be 'done' in a GCSE exam, and which can only be written about?

Laura is not certain about the inclusion of the last theme. It was something that came up in the interviews, and it surprised and interested her a lot as an idea, but she is not sure it came up in the data collection sufficiently regularly to be separately identified as a theme. She will ask her supervisor about it. Perhaps she will just incorporate it into theme 3.

Yes, she finally decides. That is what she will do. Just because it was a surprise to her does not mean it warrants being a theme in its own right.

You can see that Laura had to do a lot of spade work even before considering writing the data analysis. She cannot just collate all the information and present it in a graph or table to be analysed later. The process of analysis is to be found in identifying not who has said what, but what sorts of thing are a lot of participants saying. Before being able to start analysing any of the data, she had to make sense of it to decide how to structure it around what the main themes were. Laura will use some quotes from participants of different age groups to use as examples, but she will not use every response. That would not be possible, and there is no need to do that. Before deciding on which responses to use, she had to structure her thoughts about the data in a way that her reader will be able to engage with. You will have to do that too.

The big message here then is that if you have collected predominantly qualitative data, you should not be in too much of a rush to start organising and presenting your data or to write your data analysis. Laura took her time. She had to make sense of the data first. In order to do this (and this is where she did well) she chose initially not to look for instances of agreement. She looked instead for an overview. What did her participants talk about? What aspects of the discussions most exercised them? Whether they agreed or disagreed with each other was not Laura's interest in the early stages of her analysis. She found the themes first and then dived deeper into each later.

This is very much like the panel discussion analogy in Chapter 9 (Literature Review). You are looking to do that again in this impartial report which is your data analysis. If you were reporting on a panel discussion it would be unhelpful to your reader to just list who said what. No. That would require your reader to make sense of the overall discussion. If that reader is your assessor, they will have to do all the work for you, and of course, this would result in a poor grade. Instead, you should first identify what was being talked about. Whether speakers agreed with each other, and the reasons they gave, comes later.

The choice to separate (or not) the data from the discussion is a question of function rather than quality or style. If it makes sense to present the data and to also analyse it as you go long, then that is the best approach, and one we would recommend if your data were predominantly qualitative. If not, that is fine too. There is no right or wrong approach.

PLANNING HOW THE DATA MIGHT BE PRESENTED EVEN BEFORE COLLECTING IT

This is an advanced skill in planning and writing a research project, and very few students give this any consideration at all in the planning stages of their project. Instead, what tends to happen is that students collect data and only then try to decide what to do with it. This happened to Joachim, and his experience of writing his data analysis was not easy or successful.

Joachim was a primary trainee in Rochester, Kent. He had always struggled with satisfying Teachers' Standard 2 (Learning Environment) and so he decided to explore amongst teachers across Key Stages 1 and 2 which aspects of classroom management they found easiest and hardest, and why. His title was 'What aspects of classroom management do teachers in a primary school in North Kent find hardest, and what strategies do they adopt in these areas?'. He began by reading around the subject and collating a rather long list of fifteen aspects of classroom management: planning, resources, voice projection, indoor learning, outdoor learning, engaging with learning support assistants, furniture placement, the interactive whiteboard, noise levels, group work, individual learning, pace and timings, personalised learning, pupil autonomy, and pupil absenteeism. He thought it would be a good idea to ask the teachers to identify in a survey which of the things on the list were the most and least difficult for them using a short series of simple choice questions. He would then go on to ask them in interviews to expand upon their responses.

Joachim did not do a pilot because he felt there was not time. Seven teachers filled in the survey, and all agreed to be interviewed. The problem began for Joachim when there were no clear patterns in the survey responses. Apart from pupil absenteeism and the interactive whiteboard, which no teacher identified as challenging or not, the other thirteen aspects he had listed each attracted one or two ticks from four of the teachers as being amongst the most challenging. Unhelpfully, those same thirteen aspects also attracted one or two ticks from the other three teachers as being amongst the least challenging. How was Joachim to present that set of data? Even if he used two bar charts, one showing which aspect represented the most and the other showing the least amount of challenge, the two graphs would look pretty much the same.

Here is the source of the problem for Joachim. Without thinking about what the resulting data might look like, or what aspect of classroom management he might narrow his focus to, Joachim had simply thrown 15 aspects of classroom management at seven teachers and expected a pattern to emerge. When no pattern was forthcoming, he was disappointed. He had not considered what the data, when presented, might look like. He had not applied any filter. He had just written down everything he had previously read and experienced about effective classroom management and bundled it all into a research design with no thought at all about what would come out at the other end.

In the interviews Joachim discovered that the teachers had struggled to be confined to the choices he had given them, because they each experienced different levels of classroom management challenge in different subjects, or even from morning lessons to afternoon ones where energy levels (pupils and teachers') changed. Joachim had not considered any of this as a possibility. Two teachers who had each taught in both Key Stages reported how the challenges were different with older and younger children, and also different according to the activity. One teacher reported that even the weather could make a difference. So not only were there no interesting patterns from the survey data, the data from Joachim's interviews were also a mess as none of it fitted his neat preconception of what constituted challenge.

Prior to collecting his data, Joachim had not considered what his data might look like in terms of content or presentation. He had not anticipated what the worst-case scenario in the survey might be (and he should have done, given that there were twice as many options in the survey than people in his research population). His interview questions had intended to be based upon the survey responses, and because the survey results were so one-dimensional, they did not provide much leverage for follow up conversations either. As it happened, the interview data the teachers gave him was rich, but sadly not in a way that would answer his original research question, and certainly not as a result of the questions he had asked of them in the interviews. Joachim was lucky because his participants were experienced teachers and so they had talked about aspects and variables in classroom management, even though he had not asked them about those things directly. At least Joachim had allowed them some flexibility in the interviews, and this saved him. If he had just kept banging on about his fifteen areas in the interviews as well, it would have been a disaster.

After a panicky tutorial with his supervisor, Joachim's original question ('What aspect of classroom management do teachers in a primary school in North Kent find hardest, and what strategies do they adopt in these areas?') was adapted to read 'What range of challenging factors pertain when teachers are creating an effective learning environment?: a case study in a primary school in North Kent'. Joachim abandoned the useless survey data completely and was able to discuss the factors mentioned above using the interview data he had collected from the teachers. Joachim also wrote about this change of title, and the reasons behind it, in the conclusion chapter of his research project, to demonstrate to his marker that he had learnt a great deal about research methods, particularly data collection planning.

So again, as we have repeatedly said, there is more to getting a good grade for your research project than just answering your research question. Your demonstration of good research practice, and of your understanding of a range of aspects of that practice is also important. Despite the data collection planning disaster, Joachim secured a grade of 65%, thanks in no small part to the insight spontaneously shown by his participating teachers. It could have gone very much more badly for Joachim if the teachers had all just confined themselves to only answering the questions he was asking them. As it was, he had rich data to analyse, thanks entirely to his participants.

TABLES AND FIGURES

Tables and figures are useful when undertaking data analysis, but only if their use is appropriate. We have known students include these devices for effect, as a way of making the text of their work more varied or to make the data appear more compelling.

If you are only using them for visual effect, then we advise you not to include them, but if they can be used to present data efficiently, and to save you a lot of words in the long run, then they are very useful to include, and we recommend them.

Tables are grids of rows and columns, usually containing numbers, or sometimes with keywords (although even then there is likely to be a numeric element identifying the frequency of use of the keywords).

Figures are visual representations of something, perhaps in the form of a graph or chart, or it may be a representation of a theoretical model (for example, the two axes that make up The Simple View of Reading (Elborn, 2015: 4), or the concentric rings in the model of Bronfenbrenner's' (1979) Ecological Systems Theory.

As a rule of thumb, when it comes to presenting data, it is far more efficient to present a graph, chart, table or theoretical model than it is to try to describe its content in your text as a narrative which your reader would find impossible to engage with anyway. On no account should you do both.

Damilola is interested in questioning techniques, with a particular focus on gender. To this end he observed five Key Stage 2 teachers as they conducted introductions and plenaries to maths and literacy lessons. He made a tally of the frequency that the teachers asked direct questions to boys and girls, or the frequency of boys or girls being chosen to answer a question if they had their hands up. The teachers knew what he was observing and counting, and they were interested to know what the findings would be about their own practice.

This is a clear example where Damilola had to acknowledge in his methodology the likely presence of either Social Desirability Bias or the Hawthorne effect (Chapter 6). It is highly likely that, knowing he is making this tally, each teacher would become more aware of any potential or actual gender imbalance in their practice, and therefore would seek to minimise it whilst being observed.

The results of the observations were as follows (see Tables 10.1–10.6).

Table 10.1 Mr. Johnson. Year 3

Questioning Techniques	Answered by Girls	Answered by Boys
Direct question to an individual (Maths)	6	5
General question to the class (Maths)	2	2
Direct question to an individual (Literacy)	4	2
General question to the class (Literacy)	1	2

Table 10.2 Miss Phillips. Year 4

Questioning Techniques	Answered by Girls	Answered by Boys
Direct question to an individual (Maths)	4	3
General question to the class (Maths)	3	1
Direct question to an individual (Literacy)	3	3
General question to the class (Literacy)	0	0

Table 10.3 Mr. Shea. Year 4

Questioning Techniques	Answered by Girls	Answered by Boys
Direct question to an individual (Maths)	2	4
General question to the class (Maths)	1	0
Direct question to an individual (Literacy)	3	4
General question to the class (Literacy)	1	0

Table 10.4 Mrs. Öztürk. Year 5

Questioning Techniques	Answered by Girls	Answered by Boys
Direct question to an individual (Maths)	3	6
General question to the class (Maths)	0	1
Direct question to an individual (Literacy)	2	4
General question to the class (Literacy)	0	1

Table 10.5 Mrs. Milligan. Year 6

Questioning Techniques	Answered by Girls	Answered by Boys
Direct question to an individual (Maths)	1	0
General question to the class (Maths)	0	0
Direct question to an individual (Literacy)	3	4
General question to the class (Literacy)	1	2

Table 10.6 All Five Teachers, Combined

Questioning Techniques	Answered by Girls	Answered by Boys
Direct question to an individual (Maths)	16	18
General question to the class (Maths)	6	4
Direct question to an individual (Literacy)	15	17
General question to the class (Literacy)	3	5

The presentation of the tables (Tables 10.1–10.6) was useful to Damilola because he could demonstrate his findings clearly and concisely without the need for description. He subsequently interviewed the teachers and shared the findings with them individually (only their own data with each). Mrs Öztürk (Table 10.4) openly admitted that she had gone out of her way to involve boys whilst being observed. This was because she suspected she probably usually favoured asking questions to the girls because "you are more likely to get a sensible answer", but even so, the collection of the data was a useful lever to explore Mrs Öztürk's perceptions of her own practice and use of questions.

The observed mathematics lesson of Mrs Milligan (Table 10.5) was a recap or mastery lesson, one in which she simply modelled chunking in division, and then the children were asked to do examples individually and in pairs to reinforce their understanding. The only questioning Mrs Milligan did in that lesson was to ask a child (a girl) to explain to the class what the task was. As such, that particular lesson observation was not helpful to Damilola, but he thought it would be wrong not to report the very small tally. In this he was right. Mrs Milligan told Damilola in the interview that she intended to identify any misconceptions through her assessment of each individual undertaking of the task, rather than through questioning in which individual misconceptions can be hard to spot, so again, the seemingly thin data was able to be used to explore Mrs Milligan's professional practice.

Most of the teachers in the interviews confirmed that they rarely asked general questions to the whole class (Damilola had not realised this when he devised his method). Instead, the teachers revealed to him that they try to avoid the loss of control which can occur when lots of children put their hands up, each competing with each other to be chosen to answer. So as a policy, the teachers tend to avoid asking questions to the whole class, unless it is followed by the children being asked to discuss it with talk partners. These were not the findings Damilola expected to report when he designed his study, but he discovered all of this in the interviews through the process of tallying the frequency of questioning.

The Numbering of Tables and Figures

Damilola could have presented that information in bar charts which instead of being identified as Tables 10.1–10.6 would have been Figures 10.1–10.6 (but he was rightly careful not to present the information in both formats, as some students pointlessly do). We have numbered the tables above as Tables 10.1–10.6 because they are the first six tables in Chapter 10 of this book. Below in a later section of this chapter is a figure which is numbered Figure 10.1, not Figure 10.7 (it being the first figure in Chapter 10, even though we had previously inserted Tables 10.1–10.6). If your data analysis is Chapter 4 of your research project, the first table will be numbered Table 4.1.

FIVE THINGS TO AVOID IN DATA ANALYSIS

We list here four common errors that students make, and which weaken their submissions.

Reporting and Analysing Things That Are Not Found in Interview Data

If themes emerge in your literature review, it is likely that you will consequently expect to see those themes manifesting themselves in some way in the interview data you collect. It could well be that after undertaking and listening to your interviews, however, you come to realise that none of your participants mentioned or implied anything about one or more of the themes. This is fine and need not worry you. Indeed, this would be a feature of your data, and one which you can mention, albeit briefly, towards the end of your data analysis, perhaps in the conclusion. But although it is a feature of your data, it is not a finding from your data, and therefore it is not something that you should actively include in your analysis. If you have interviewed people, you should report and analyse what was said, and you should not make a big thing about what was not said, because that would be an example of you imposing yourself on the data. In that situation, the lens of your analysis would be your expectations of what the participants 'should' have said, and so in the eyes of your marker you would have lost all sense of neutrality.

Participants failing to say things that you were expecting is not the same thing as a nil response or a non-response. A nil response occurs when you ask a direct question, such as 'How often do you use different coloured pens when marking children's work?' and the answer is 'zero' or perhaps 'no' or 'never'. A non-response occurs when you ask a question or ask participants to engage in a task or a survey question, and they are unwilling or unable to do so.

If nothing was said about a theme that you identified as important in your literature review, there is no need to go back to the literature review and remove that theme. The literature review identifies what was found in the literature, not what should or might be found in your data. In this respect, your literature review is independent of your data analysis. If participants do not raise the things you were expecting, this is not problematic for you.

Gemma, an Early Years trainee in a setting in Bath, interviewed teachers about their early morning routines. Amongst other organisational things, she was trying to get a sense of their mental state at the start of each day before the children arrived, mainly because Gemma herself was a torrent of rush and panic on each and every school day morning, and she wanted to know whether this was the norm, and if not, what was the secret that enabled teachers to relax a bit. So, in addition to asking two teachers in her current school, and two from her first placement, about the logistics of their mornings, she asked them to speak about their mood before the children arrived. She then counted the keywords they each used (see Table 10.7), which were very revealing.

Table 10.7 Frequency of Keywords Relevant to Teachers' State of Mind

Words Relating to ...	Miss Lewis	Mr Minhas	Mrs Daynor	Mrs Marfo
Excited or motivated	1	3	2	4
Calm	2	1	2	2
Resources or materials	6	4	8	6
Organisation or management	7	6	8	4
Prior success or positive experience	5	5	4	4
Panic, worry, or anxious	0	0	0	0

Gemma was able to report that all the teachers were extremely organised. They knew from experience that if their resources were prepared, and their classroom management was consistent, things were likely to go well. As a result, they could all use positive words to describe their state of mind.

Gemma should not have reported the zero incidents of the key words 'panic', 'anxious', or 'worry' in Table 10.2, words which none of the teachers used. In reporting all these zeros, and by adding a self-interested category of analysis into which none of the data fell, she demonstrated the extent to which she overtly imposed her own attitudes on the data analysis. Had even one teacher said something along those lines, then she could have included it in the table if it was important to that one teacher's experience. Gemma had wanted to demonstrate how the mental state of the teachers in the mornings differed so radically from her own experiences, but she was very wrong to do so because the research project was not about her. Sadly, there were other examples in her data analysis where she allowed herself to become a lens through which she analysed the data. She should have consistently related the responses to the findings she presented in her literature review, not to her own experiences and attitudes. This serious error negatively affected her grade, and she was disappointed with 52%.

Over- and Under-Interrogation of the Data

If you are new to data analysis, you will lack the experience to know how hard to make the data work for you. The skill is getting a balance between over- and under-interrogation of the data. At one end of the spectrum, we have seen students who seek to apply every analytic model they can find on each and every scrap of data, wringing the data dry, and in so doing making so many claims on behalf of the data that some or most of the claims are unsupportable. At the other end of the scale are those students who give so little attention to the variations, agreements, consistencies or inconsistencies contained in their data that they fail to notice or report significant features of it. The data appears to be just a fog of information to them, and they do not, or perhaps cannot, see any patterns or synergies contained there.

For example, Joy was a secondary Maths trainee. After leaving school with 'A' Levels she had worked for a short time in a data analysis department of a well-known insurance company before changing career to train as a teacher. Thinking that in her research project it would be a good idea to draw upon the skills and knowledge she gained during her previous experience, Joy asked a series of questions using Likert scales designed to generate exclusively quantitative data (for example, 'To what extent to you agree with these statements on a scale from 1–5'). In an unashamedly brazen attempt to impress her supervisor, it was Joy's intention to then expose that data to ANOVA (Analysis of Variance) tests, correlation tests, regression models, computation of Cronbach's alpha coefficients, the calculation of standard deviations, and the identification of bivariate associations. Do not worry if you have not even heard of some of those things, because Joy's supervisor had not heard of some of them either. Joy had done well to recruit ten teachers in her examination of her research question, which was 'What aspects of the UK secondary maths curriculum do teachers in a school in East Sussex find hardest to teach, and which aspects do they think children find hardest to learn? Are these aspects the same?' It is true there is a lot going on in that question, but since Joy had chosen a mainly quantitative route to answer it, all she felt she needed to do was to identify through tables or graphs what patterns appeared in the Likert scale responses, and to identify where there was agreement amongst the ten participants and where consensus was absent or less obvious. It is true that if Joy had collected a huge amount of data, involving hundreds of participants, she might apply one of these models to her quantitative data, but her intention to apply all of them to what was a very limited amount of data constituted a misunderstanding on Joy's part of what is, and what is not, an appropriate level of analysis. And even if she did use one of the models, how does an identification of standard deviation help Joy to identify which aspects of the maths curriculum teachers in a school in East Sussex think children find hardest to learn? It doesn't. To explore the fundamentals of her research question, there is no need for Joy to go there. Joy made the mistake of assuming that when it comes to quantitative data analysis, more is better. She also was in error in assuming that impressing a supervisor with her knowledge of data analysis models was more important than demonstrating she could undertake a research project appropriately or could answer her research question.

By contrast, and at the other end of the spectrum, Morag undertook her final placement in a school which advocated a Forest School approach. She interviewed four Key Stage 2 teachers and two Key Stage 1 teachers about their attitudes and perceptions concerning Forest schooling. She collated the data in three themes drawn from her literature review (the scope for children's development including cognitive, social, emotional, and physical aspects; the pedagogical approach of Forest schools; and the challenges and tensions encountered in their implementation) and within those three themes Morag simply reported what each individual teacher had said. Morag took such a light touch to the data that she made no attempt to analyse the data as a cohort of six participants. She made no connections and identified no differences between their responses. Even though she had used her literature review to generate the three themes that she attempted to shoehorn the responses into, there was very little reference to her literature review within her data analysis chapter in order to identify the extent to which the views of her six participants individually or collectively resonated with the themes contained in the literature surrounding Forest schools. In short, although Morag accurately reported what the individual teachers had said, there was no attempt to analyse the responses or to make sense of them, no attempt to apply the responses to her literature review, and no attempt to find patterns within the data, when there were lots of opportunities to do so. She reported, but did not analyse, and in so doing she seriously under-interrogated the data.

Seeking and Reporting Only the Data that Confirm Your Preconceptions

This is a very common and costly mistake. The students who make this error tend to assume that any data they collect which does not fit or support their expectations is either unhelpful or dangerous and should therefore be ignored. These students think, very incorrectly, that if they fail to positively answer their research question, this could result in a poor grade or even failure, so they seek out, report and amplify responses that match their expectations, and they actively disregard everything else. Put like that, you can see that this is very poor research practice indeed.

Terri conducted her research project with Year 3 children, and she was convinced that if she played gentle background music when children were engaged in writing activities, this would improve both concentration and behaviour management. As a result, she anticipated that the writing that the children produced would be better (or at least there would be more of it). Terri was certain of this because when she was writing her own essays, she always had music playing in the background. She liked it and she felt that it helped. Terri intended to compare two pieces of writing from each of the children – one written without background music, and a subsequent one written with. She would then compare the two pieces of writing using two criteria: firstly, the number of words produced, and secondly, the quality of the writing measured in use of adjectives (which was the learning intention). She would then interview some of the children about their experiences. There is nothing wrong with that research design in and of itself, but Terri's application of it was very skewed.

For example, Terri reported the positive finding that of the 25 pupils who agreed to take part, fourteen produced more words when music was playing than when it was not. She did not report that of the nine who produced fewer words, six produced significantly fewer, and one pupil, Xander, produced next to nothing when previously he had been quite prolific. Regarding the use of adjectives, Terri reported that 22 of the 25 pupils used at least one adjective during the session with music. Previously, and without the music, eighteen had used adjectives. Terri did not disclose whether the additional four pupils had previously been part of the six non-adjective-users. Was it possible that some who previously used adjectives now did not when the music was playing? Terri did not say.

When Terri interviewed the children, she claimed to use 'purposive sampling', in that she chose from amongst the fourteen (thus, only from those children who had seemingly benefitted from the background music). Unsurprisingly, Terri collected and reported data which suggested almost universal approval from the children. How could the data suggest anything else? Surely, if Terri was allowing herself to use purposive sampling, it would have been more instructive (and professionally interesting) to have interviewed Xander, who produced next to nothing when the background music was playing, and from amongst the other eight who produced fewer words second time round. But no. It is not that Terri had considered it to be a risk if she interviewed those children who produced less. It was worse than that. She was so interested in demonstrating the positive effects of background music that it did not even occur to her to explore the opposite side of her argument. She was so interested in demonstrating the positive effects of background music it had never once crossed her mind that good research endeavours to explore and illuminate all facets of a research question. This is because it had never occurred to Terri that music could serve as a significant distraction for some pupils.

Terri's method served to hinder and narrow her data collection. Had she chosen instead a method in which she only interviewed a selection of children, without undertaking all the quantitative aspects, she would have heard from a cross section of children, rather than just those who produced more words under the influence of background music. In doing so she is likely to have heard responses that countered her preconception, made her research project much more nuanced, and may also have informed her future professional practice as a result. She may even have interviewed Xander, who perhaps would have held strong views. As it is Terri will now go on to embark upon her future career firm in the knowledge that background music when children are writing is a good and generally helpful thing. Poor Xander. He used to love writing.

Her supervisor and her second marker each noticed that there was an absence of non corroborating data in Terri's submission. Terri only reported data that supported her preconception (her hypothesis). She ignored any consideration of anything that countered it, and even actively avoided the chance to delve into the experiences of those who might offer an alternative view. To an experienced marker this looks very odd and suspicious indeed and if you choose to take such an uncritical approach, this could very easily affect your grade. The chances of collecting data in which there are no conflicting voices are very remote.

You are advised, therefore, to celebrate a range of responses, and report them. Seek them out and try to test your research question. If it turns out that your data suggests that (for example) background music makes very little difference to children's work, or is distracting, or serves to completely scupper some children's ability to write anything at all, that is a perfectly good discovery, and is an informed answer to your question. The fact that it is not the answer you were expecting is not the point. You are not saying that your answer is the case with all children everywhere. You are just saying that for the participants in your particular study, these (plural) outcomes or attitudes were the range that were found. You are also demonstrating that the scope of your findings was not confined by the limits of your own preconceptions.

Misuse of Graphs

This is a very frequent error. Figure 10.1 displays two graphs, each purportedly showing the same thing, but one presents the data incorrectly. They are each trying to show how many different types of punctuation were contained in each of four children's written work.

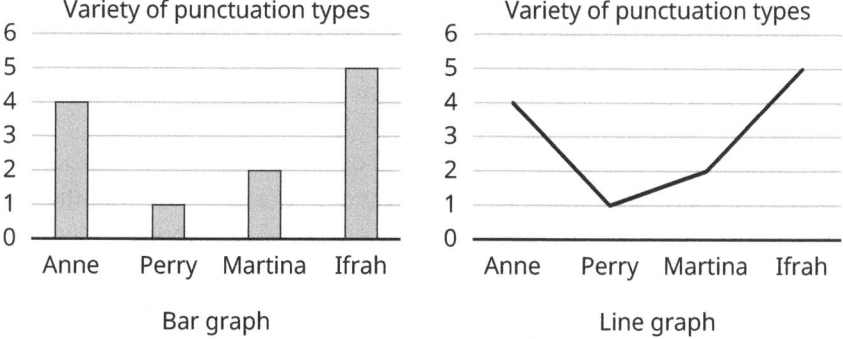

Figure 10.1 Appropriate and Inappropriate Presentation of Tally Information

The bar graph is correct for these data. The names of the children and the corresponding bars could have been presented in any order, and there is no implied connection between any of the columns.

The line graph is incorrect. A line graph suggests sequence, and the line itself constitutes the depiction of sequential connected multiple data points, often representing time or gradual development, so each point along the line should represent development or change or relationship between preceding and subsequent points. Obviously, that is impossible and unwelcome in this case, because there is no sequential connection between the values of Ann, Perry, Martina and Ifrah's punctuation use. The presentation of a point of the line graph depicting a value of 1.5 halfway between Perry and Martina is worse than irrelevant. It is meaningless nonsense. Nonetheless, we have seen this erroneous use of line graphs very often. Such misuse of graphs will not seriously affect your grade (unless perhaps you are a trainee maths teacher and your research project has a maths focus, in which case you deserve to be penalised), but it lets down the authenticity of your work. It discloses a naivety in your mathematical understanding, which is obviously not a good thing when presenting quantitative data.

Describing Graphs and Charts

A sure sign that a student does not have enough to say about their data is if they describe as a narrative the contents of a graph. The function of a graph is to save your word count. It presents data in a visually succinct and accessible way. There is absolutely nothing to be gained from presenting a graph and then saying what figures or values the graph contains. Do not do it. Your marker can see from a graph that (for example in Figure 10.1) Ann used four different types of punctuation in her writing, Martina used two, Ifrah five and Perry, only one. If you choose to tell your marker that after presenting the graph, this constitutes nineteen words you did not need to use, and your marker will also feel patronised as a result. That is a lose-lose situation for you.

SUMMARY

The main points we hope you have taken form this chapter are as follows:

- It is a strong thing to do to consider how you might present your data before collecting it.
- Look for the big headlines or patterns in the data you collect. First, what are most people talking about? Second, to what extent do they agree with each other?
- You should only report things that your data show. Do not report nil returns regarding things that your data did not show, but which you were expecting to see.
- It does not matter whether your data fits in well with your literature. Your job is to identify the extent to which patterns in your data are found or are not found in the literature. You do not have to make it fit (indeed, you must not even try to do that. That would be manipulation).

- Getting the balance right between over- and under-analysis of your data can be tricky, and is not an exact science, but if you are extracting every ounce of possible meaning from a limited amount of data, your conclusions will not be valid. Look for the big headlines. Do not try to mine every last nugget of possible meaning from the responses of your participants.
- Look to be surprised. Embrace responses that do not fit with your initial expectations. Report responses that do not agree. Learn to enjoy any incongruity found within your data.

FURTHER READING

Bergin, T. (2018). *An introduction to data analysis: Quantitative, qualitative and mixed methods.* London: SAGE.

This book offers a complete introduction to the fundamentals of data analysis. Using real-world case studies as illustrations, it helps readers understand theories behind and develop techniques for conducting quantitative, qualitative, and mixed methods data analysis.

Blaikie, N. (2003). *Analyzing quantitative data.* London: SAGE.

This book is designed for social researchers who need to know what procedures to use under what circumstances, in practical research projects.

Silverman, D. (2024). *Interpreting qualitative data.* 7th edn. London: SAGE.

This book gives you the practical grounding in qualitative methods you need to get started especially if you are new to qualitative research or conducting your first research project in the social sciences.

REFERENCES

Bronfenbrenner, U. (1979) *The ecology of human development.* Harvard University Press.

Elborn, S. (2015) *Handbook of teaching early reading: More than phonics.* Leicester: UKLA. ISBN: 13:978–1–897638–98–9

11

LAST STEPS: THE CONCLUSION, THE INTRODUCTION, THE ABSTRACT, AND THE PROOFREADING

―――――――――― **Chapter Aims** ――――――――――

- Why the conclusion matters.
- Key elements of a strong conclusion.
- Mistakes to avoid in a conclusion.
- Examples of conclusion styles, of different levels of quality.
- Key elements of a strong introduction, and why the introduction is likely to be the last chapter you write.
- Key elements of an abstract.

INTRODUCTION

This chapter has a curious structure, in that it considers the conclusion, the introduction and the abstract in that order, and then also explores the (too often) overlooked necessity of proofreading. We have chosen this approach because in our experience, this is the most useful and rational order to undertake these sections of your research project. They are considered so late in that book because we recommend that they are the last sections you write.

WHY THE CONCLUSION MATTERS

For many students, and you may be one of them, the conclusion is one of the hardest chapters to write. If you are not clear in your own mind what you are trying to achieve in a conclusion chapter, it will obviously be impossible to know whether you have been successful. For this reason, you may have struggled with conclusions in every essay you have written, because in your previous submissions you had already been careful to say everything you wanted to say about a subject, and now your university expects you to conclude as well. Surely, you argue, this is just repetition? Some students struggle so much that their submissions or essays just stop with a shuddering halt with no conclusion at all, either because the student had run out of wordcount, or time, or because they had no idea what a good conclusion looks like or what it should contain.

But a conclusion is not just repetition. There are skills and conventions in finishing any form of human communication, whether it be a letter, a book, a film, a play, an essay, or an evening with friends, and none of these involves the simple repetition of what was previously said. In any of these examples, it would be rude, awkward or odd to suddenly just stop communicating once you felt everything had been communicated. You will know deep down of course that any submission without a conclusion leads to a very unsatisfying finish for you and for your reader, because an academic submission is not only about content. It is about communication, persuasion, and clarity too. This chapter is intended to give you the ideas and perspective you need to finish your research project with a strong and satisfying conclusion.

Key Elements of a Strong Conclusion

A strong research project conclusion has many constituent parts, and you should allow about 10% of your total wordcount to it. It restates the research aim or question, summarises the main findings, discusses the implications of the study, and identifies the extent to which the study resonates with the literature of the field. It acknowledges the methodological or contextual limitations of the study, but not in an apologetic or overly critical way as some students do. There is no need to adopt false modesty and take a hatchet to your research project by completely dismissing its scale and methodology, thus suggesting it is not worthy of the name. A strong conclusion will also suggest future research foci (perhaps questions that arose for you during the undertaking of your study but which you had not thought of before and which you did not have the scope to include), and it will identify things that you have learnt along the way (not only about your research question, but you should also identify things you have learnt about research methods, or research vocabulary, ethics or data collection and analysis). That is a lot to write about, and since we recommend your conclusion should constitute about 10% of your submission, in a 6,000–8,000-word submission you would only have 600–800 words to do it in, so you must be concise.

Before writing your own conclusion, as an exercise we recommend that either individually or with some fellow students you take a short research report (perhaps a journal article) and once you reach the heading 'Conclusion' stop reading and try to identify what the main points are, how the writer came to their conclusion, why the writer considered those points be compelling and important, and what the implications of these key findings might be for professional practice. In short you are planning the conclusion on the part of the author. It would then be interesting to see the extent to which your perceptions of the key points align with that of the author. They may not, but that is not the issue. The important thing is the ability to be able to take an overview.

This skill is important because in a conclusion you are identifying to your marker your perceptions of the key points, and their implications. Whether your marker agrees with you about your choices is not very important. Your marker wants to see that you can take an overview and that you can concisely identify and present what you consider to be the headlines from your study, both methodological and analytical, and show why they are compelling, and what their implications might be, and for whom or what.

Mistakes to Avoid in a Conclusion

The conclusion sits on top of everything else, supported by what has gone before. It is not there to look nice, like the icing on a cake, but it is there to bring the research project to a satisfying finish. There should be no surprises in a conclusion, no new information about your research question, no new perspectives on the data.

Students can fall foul of a variety of stylistic and content errors in a conclusion. The most common are that some students simply repeat their introduction, in effect saying identical things in the two chapters but by rephrasing. Others finish with an abrupt ending, saying what they want to say and then just stopping with a jolt when everything has been said or when the wordcount runs out. This discloses a lack of awareness of the needs or experience of the reader. Some students add new findings or discussion in the conclusion that had not been included in the data analysis, and this is a big error, because this shows a lack of analysis, or at least an incompleteness, in the first place.

You should also avoid making overstated claims about your data or about aspects of your design. Your study may suggest things, but it does not prove anything, and you must not make such a claim. Your study may well support the themes found in your literature review (equally it may not), but this does not mean the literature contains truth. Be very cautious about using phrases such as '... the fact is ...', ... 'my study shows' ... or 'it can therefore be seen'. As researchers become more experienced, the language and vocabulary they use to conclude their studies tends to become increasingly tentative. Do not make claims or suggest insights that the data does not safely support.

Two Examples of Conclusions, One Strong, One Less So

Below are the research project conclusion chapters of two students, Freda and Karin. Both students explored aspects of the role of Teaching Assistants in primary classrooms. It is likely that you will judge Karin's conclusion to be much more effective than Freda's, but after you have read them, and before we go on to identify the strengths or limitations of each, please stop to identify to yourself specifically why one is so much stronger than the other.

Example 1: Freda's Conclusion

This research aimed to find out whether teaching assistants (TAs) are effective in the primary classroom. I interviewed some teachers and TAs and also observed some lessons. I found that TAs can help children with their learning and support the teacher. They were especially useful when working with children in small groups. Some teachers said they wouldn't cope without their TA.

Overall, I think TAs are very important and should be in every class. They can help pupils understand the work and keep them on task. They also make the teacher's job easier. From what I saw, they are doing a good job. I think more schools should have more TAs.

There were a few limitations in this research. I only looked at one school and didn't have much time to observe all the classes. Also, I didn't ask pupils what they thought, which might have given me more insight.

In the future, more research could be done in other schools to see if the same things happen there. It might also be useful to ask parents or headteachers what they think about TAs.

Overall, I believe that TAs are helpful in classrooms and can improve education.

Example 2: Karin's Conclusion

This research set out to explore the question: *In what ways can Teaching Assistants be effective in the primary classroom?* Drawing on interviews with class teachers and TAs, alongside classroom observations, the findings indicate that TAs can be highly effective, particularly in supporting individual learners and small groups. However, their effectiveness is strongly dependent on the quality of planning, communication, and direction provided by the class teacher.

These findings from the data collected from the interviews suggest that schools could not only invest in the deployment of TAs but also in professional development for teachers and TAs alike, focusing on how to integrate TAs purposefully into lesson planning. Without this strategic planning, TAs risk being underutilised or used in ways that do not support learning outcomes.

The extent to which the combined responses of the participants resonated with the literature of the field was mixed. That is because the literature can be divided on the effectiveness of TAs in either their deployment or in their utilisation according to which research is read.

While the study was limited by its small sample size and single-school context, it contributes to ongoing discussions about the value of TAs in inclusive education. Future research could examine the long-term impact of structured TA/teacher collaboration on pupil engagement, and across diverse key stages.

In conclusion, TAs are not inherently effective or ineffective – their impact depends on the systems and support around them. This research reinforces the idea that effective deployment of TAs must be an intentional part of school practice.

In hindsight, if I were to undertake this study again, I think it would have been more effective to separate the TAs and the teachers more obviously, both in the questions that were asked and the way the data was presented. Throughout the research project the two groups were treated as one homogenous cohort of professional educationalists. The same questions were asked of each, but it was only when I came to analyse the data I realised that it would have been more illustrative to have asked some separate questions, at least towards the end of the interviews.

A key thing I have learnt about undertaking research in a school setting is the importance of devising questions which give participants the freedom to articulate their own views on a subject, wherever that leads. With the help of my supervisor, I amended my original intended questions to allow participants much more freedom in the areas they spoke about. As a result, many participants responded in ways I had not previously thought of, and about things I had not considered, and this allowed me to broaden my perspective, and adapt my research question. Also, regarding good research practice, I was surprised to learn the wide range of factors that must be taken into account when considering research ethics, and as a result I now have a much more realistic and developed understanding of what educational research involves.

Everyone who was involved enjoyed this research project. Certainly, I benefitted from it, and my own professional engagement with TAs in my future career will be enhanced and informed by it. Many of the participants also said how much they enjoyed and benefitted from the opportunity to reflect on what they do and why, individually and together, and their priorities when doing them. Several TAs remarked unsolicited that they felt valued as a result of taking part in the study. The whole thing has been a positive experience for all concerned.

Reasons Why Karin's Conclusion Is Stronger Than Freda's

Both conclusions revisit different aspects of the project, and refer to further research, but there are five aspects or omissions of Freda's work which mean her conclusion is undeveloped, ineffective, and very short.

First, there is no restatement of the research question or indication as to why it was a compelling one to ask. You can imagine that a research project is a big and time-consuming thing to assess, and markers rarely read an entire research project in one uninterrupted go. It is entirely possible that in between chapters your tutor will have gone off to teach or engage in a meeting, so it is good practice to start each chapter with a reminder about your research question.

Second, the conclusion is too general and vague ("TAs are helpful" … they are "doing a good job"). Freda seems to be doing no more in her conclusion than vaguely generalising about TAs everywhere. Her research does not feature compellingly. It is evident that Freda approves of Teaching Assistants, but it is not clear in her conclusion what aspects of her study support such approval, and why, or for what. The research project that Freda undertook is rather incidental to this conclusion.

Third, following from the previous criticism, Freda's conclusion is very much about Freda. The word 'I' appears in almost every paragraph. Yes, Karin uses 'I' too and talks about her own professional and academic development towards the end of her conclusion, but for Freda, the whole of the conclusion is very much an expression of her thoughts about the efficacy of Teaching Assistants. Freda's conclusion lacks an academic voice, most keenly evidenced by phrases such as 'I did...' . 'I think... 'and 'I believe...'. the conclusion should be much more about what her participants do, think and believe, not Freda. The evidence from this conclusion is that Freda appears to have come through her research project without being influenced, informed or affected by it in any way.

Fourth, Freda simply revisits her findings and method through description, not analysis or synthesis. For example, there is no summary of key findings, or any reference to the literature, with a reminder of the extent to which the main themes in the literature resonate with the responses of her participants.

The fifth oversight in Freda's conclusion is there is no critical reflection on the 'conditions' that might pertain which would contribute to TA effectiveness. For Freda, TAs are inherently a good thing. There is no consideration or identification as to what factors her participants thought might enhance or restrict TA effectiveness, or what they considered the parameters of the TA's role to be. It is all very stated, vague, and general, and leaves the reader asking, 'Is that it? Are these bland comments the limit of Freda's big take-aways from this study?'.

By contrast, Karin's conclusion is much more satisfying as a finish to a research project because it cements the reader's sense of her understanding of the field, and the place of her research project within that field. Such a confident conclusion to the research project will enhance Karin's grade because she demonstrates that she has a good degree of mastery over her subject. She restates the research question clearly and summarises and applies her study's key findings (but without repeating the entire discussion). The conclusion is tightly focused on Karin's' research project, not Karin's preconceptions, centring as it does on the project's findings and processes. This is vital in a strong conclusion. Karin's conclusion is not simply idle conjecture about the place of TAs, as Freda's conclusion is. Karin's conclusion is tightly clamped to previous chapters.

Karin also reflects on some implications for practice (for example about teacher development) and considers the extent to which the views of her participants resonate with the main themes of her literature review. She acknowledges the limitations of her study (but without apologising for them) and suggests ways in which the study might have been improved in hindsight. Additionally, she suggests an interesting focus for future research and includes some thought-provoking insight tying the whole study together. Karin identifies what she has learnt from a methodological point of view in the light of her experience of undertaking research, and the conclusion finishes with a gentle hoorah which gives a real sense of accomplishment and a clear feel-good factor.

Karin's conclusion brings her research project to a very satisfying finish. Like any long journey, having reached their destination together, Karin and her marker can both now disembark and say their farewells having shared an agreeable journey together, during which Karin has shared insights about things that have interested them both. That is the role of the conclusion. It is not a parting hug, but it is a warm professional hand-shake where Karin and her marker can metaphorically look each other in the eye and the marker can say, 'Well done, I can see your understanding'.

KEY ELEMENTS OF A STRONG INTRODUCTION, AND WHY THE INTRODUCTION IS LIKELY TO BE THE LAST CHAPTER YOU WRITE

It is ironic that our consideration of the Introduction to your research project comes towards the end of this book, but in our experience, that is the order in which things are done, and it is the order we recommend you do it. It is highly likely that somewhere during the process of the research project your best-laid plans will change at least a little, and sometimes, a lot. This might be because of advice from your supervisor, or from unexpected changes of direction once you start to involve participants (or choose not to), or perhaps from unexpected obstacles or opportunities regarding participants, the research setting, or data collection. It would be very inefficient to write an introductory chapter about where your research project is going before you knew for sure where it went. You are therefore likely to be writing the conclusion and the introduction at similar times.

The introduction should ease your reader gently into the submission, just as your conclusion should be a gentle exit. Like your methodology it should be written in the past tense, because your research project is a report, identifying what you did, not what you intend to do. That is another reason for writing the introduction towards the end of your project.

Your introduction should not only identify the research question, but you should also explain why it has been chosen. To this end, within the first half of this chapter you are allowed a degree of personality and self within your project for the first and last time. What experiences have brought you to this point? Why does this research question interest you? What aspects of your professional development are you hoping the project will develop? (You might revisit this in your conclusion). For example, Louis has a keen interest in Music which influenced his decision to explore synergies between pedagogies in primary school Music and Maths. By contrast, Sukanya is a first-generation immigrant, arriving in the UK from India speaking Punjabi and stilted English aged 10, and is interested in the experiences of secondary school children with English as an Additional Language. As a third example, Poppy struggles with classroom management and wants to use her research project to explore this area of professional development. They each mention these things in their introductions (but not to any great length).

In addition to presenting the research question and your reasons for being interested in it, you might also identify your positionality, which means stating your pre-conceptions. This is to guard against bias. Do not worry. By doing this you are not asking for trouble by admitting bias. There is no such thing as entirely unbiased research, because even your choice of question is a demonstration of your predilection for that subject or field. Obviously, you have an interest in your focus of study, else you would not have chosen it. By implication you probably hold views or attitudes towards the subject, however loosely formed or strongly held. But by stating your positionality, you are demonstrating that you are aware that your study cannot be value-free. To return to Louis, he has long wondered whether teaching Year 2 children to write and clap musical notation with its breves, semibreves, minims, crotchets, and quavers, each being half as long as its predecessor in the list, might help the children to understand fractions, specifically halves and quarters, and its inverse of doubling (this is his hypothesis, and speaks of his knowledge and interest in the field). Louis does not intend to test the children doing fractions before and after teaching them the notation or indeed to do anything that would generate quantitative data because he is more interested in exploring the children's learning experiences than in measuring their progress. He does not want his project boiled down to a collection of numeric data (another disclosed aspect of his positionality, this time about method). He would prefer to teach the children these musical notations and then just talk to them about their experiences of learning to read the notes, and of doubling and halving. He wants to hear their perceptions of learning, and whether they think the music notation helps with the fractions, and how enjoyable it was, learning in this way. So, Louis discloses this in his introduction, but again, not at any great length. The project is not about Louis. Once this section of the introduction is finished, Louis will not appear in his research project again until possibly and briefly at the very end of the conclusion (as in Karin's conclusion, above). Neither will you.

Your introduction will go on to briefly herald the key themes in your literature review. The themes need only be listed, not explored (that will come in the literature review itself). You will also reveal what research methods your study used (but not why, that will come in the methodology), and you should also simply state the key themes that emerged from the data (but do not offer any explanations or implications. They will come in the data analysis and the conclusion respectively). There is no recommended minimum wordcount to an introduction but if it is longer than about 800 words you might consider making it more concise. The important thing is that it should clearly announce the direction of travel and identify your rationale for undertaking the study in the first place.

KEY ELEMENTS OF AN ABSTRACT

Check whether your institution requires your research project to be headed by an abstract, but it is most likely that it will. The word comes from the Latin *abstractum*, (abs = 'take away' or 'removed', tract = text). In effect an abstract is the separation of key points from a larger text. In the same way we also get 'contract' (con = coming together) and 'extract' (ex = out of).

Abstracts have been likened to the blurb on the back of a book, but this is only partially true, and this is a very unhelpful analogy for your research project. The blurb on a book is designed to encourage a reader to read the book, but it will invariably include a cliffhanger, so the author's big plot reveal is hidden and there is no spoiler. That is the absolute opposite of what an abstract should contain. Abstracts are so useful to researchers because when looking for sources, particularly journal articles, there should be enough information in an abstract to tell you everything you need to know about a published paper so that you can decide whether it is likely to be useful to you, but all usually within about 150–200 words. This would include research focus, method, size (number of participants) outcomes and headline implications. It will not include ethics, as that is a given and should be explored within the paper or article. But even so, that is a lot of information to get into 150 words, so abstracts tend to be very dense, highly factual, and as a result very hard to write.

You should avoid making claims of self-endorsement in your abstract such as "This study includes a comprehensive literature review …" or "The data were subjected to in-depth analysis…". Your marker will be the judge of how comprehensive your literature is, or the depth of your analysis, and these are not phrases that are used in published abstracts.

Below are example abstracts from four dissertations. The first is from a published article from one of the authors of this book, and the others are examples of students abstracts. You will not need to copy or closely adapt the content of these abstracts, but you should try to replicate the style. Please note the convention is that abstracts are written in the third person and presented in italics. The italics are not entirely compulsory, but the use of the third person is a given.

This study explores how a cohort of fifteen teaching assistants, mentors and trainee teachers perceive the practice of the deployment of teaching assistants during a school experience on an Initial Teacher Training programme in southeast London. A qualitative research approach based on an interpretivist paradigm was used through the lens of Bourdieu's theory of habitus, capital and field. This was utilized to determine whether trainee teachers found the nature of deployment of teaching assistants difficult owing to a struggle for power within the classroom. Data were collected through questionnaires and semi-structured interviews.

Analysis revealed that trainee teachers in this study have the perception that the habitus of their school environment is one in which they recognize aspects of having little control. They are expected to conform to the expectations of the schools' habitus and teach in accordance with the existing pedagogy. There exists a perception of some practice replicating existing pedagogy and a resignation that autonomy is sacrificed at the expense of fitting into the system required within a school.

Trainee teachers recognize the right to deploy their teaching assistants but appear not to wish to engage in an overt struggle for power – but rather do it subtly, by preferring to adopt a process of 'localized familiarization'. This, in their perception, enables them to work towards 'equality' in the classroom through negotiation and discussion. What is revealed, however, is a surprising amount of power wielded by the teaching assistant who may be viewed as a monitor of the habitus.

(Morgan, 2019)

Finally, here are three examples of abstracts from students' undergraduate dissertations. Saffron wrote:

This project explores the relationship between physical exercise and children's well-being in Key Stage one. The project focuses on the amount of physical exercise carried out by a year 1 class of twenty-six children in timetabled lessons as well as organised play time and associated activities, for example, the daily mile. The research was conducted as action research over a period of one academic term, with data collected in the form of observations and self-administered questionnaires, for example a well-being index. From the collected data the researcher suggested that physical exercise is beneficial to perceived levels of positive well-being, but it is important to note how children perceive their well-being in a school day.

Aaron's abstract read as follows:

This case study project explores the perceptions of teachers in a primary school based in Hull towards taking pupils to visit community libraries whilst exploring the strategies used to promote and support collaboration between the school and the library hubs. In total, eight members of staff from the primary school and four members of the library hub staff participated in the research. Data were collected from the participants in the form of semi-structured interview.

Interpreted data indicated that many of the teachers perceived time and risk assessment as being barriers to either wanting to visit libraries or implementing learning gained from such visits in an already crowded curriculum.

Many suggested strategies were realised across the school to encourage the visits to the library hub to enhance children's learning and development. Data showed that the school favoured collaborative opportunities with librarians, and tracking data showed some benefit of the visits. The library staff's perspective was that visits from local primary schools enabled staff to consider the provision of reading books on offer and would help with visitor numbers to help secure further local government funding.

Hofesh wrote:

This small-scale study aimed to investigate undergraduate, trainee teachers' experiences of confidence during their primary education studies at a university in West Wales. The level of confidence largely explored is the ability to feel secure in responding to lecturer's questions in teaching sessions (focussing on lecture and seminar spaces) and volunteering questions in discussions. This research is particularly informed by the literature regarding student populations; and general anxiety with society, as well as the observations of me as a student and being in receipt of many of my peers saying how uneasy they were in being asked questions in a public space.

Questionnaires, with a high use of Likert scales, were sent out to 90 final year trainees. Twelve responses were returned, one male and eleven female, in this study of the whole final year cohort. Ten of these respondents volunteered to participate in a lengthy semi-structured interview.

The analysis found that most trainees in the study experienced a lack of confidence and that their levels of confidence were not necessarily affected by what they knew, but what they thought of how others would judge what they knew (or did not know). To that extent it was suggested that many students would actively not seek to engage with a lecturer's questioning or feel shy in table-based discussions. The research suggests that the confidence levels of students would increase if they could demonstrate their understanding by large scale participation methods such as Mentimeter or Kahoot!, so that anonymity could guarantee approval, before having any confidence to speak in public.

THE NECESSITY OF PROOFREADING

Proofreading is essential and is a skill that should not be skimped. If you were going to a formal event, you would expect to follow the dress code, and this would involve putting quite a bit of thought and effort in. Your host would expect it, and had you not bothered to look smart you would be very conspicuous. Your research project is that formal event, and proof proofreading is your thought and effort. It is the public-facing aspect of your work, that represents and signifies not only your research but the person who wrote it. (Did you spot the double use of the word 'proof' in the previous sentence? If not, then this is why proofreading matters). Proofreading is not easy. Some would say it is impossible to proofread your own work because you are anticipating what is coming, and not reading what is actually on the page, as your marker will be. You cannot afford to put in months of hard work only to present text that contains typos (typographical errors), vaguely composed sentences, outright mistakes or formatting errors. Proofreading, therefore, is the timely skill of carefully checking your writing before a public submission to avoid some degree of doubt from your reader.

Proofreading matters because it represents a degree of professionalism; it shows care has gone into the crafting of your final draft and that the revised edits have enabled you to present the polished version. It provides your work with clarity. Just because you know what you mean it does not necessarily follow that your reader will know what you mean.

A good tip is to allow a lay person to read your work and to receive a good understanding of what your work means; this can be a family member or a good friend. If they ask too many questions about your meaning, then you know that a revision is required. It is also a good idea to read your work out loud from a hard copy. You will see and hear many errors you had not previously noticed when reading in your head from a screen.

When it comes to the data you will need to be accurate because flawed data equals a flawed research project and that will not do. Check the data, check the analysis and check the reporting of the findings. In fact, 'check everything' is a sensible mantra for the proofreading element of your work. Check your work against the marking criteria, or when you do further research – check the requirements of the publisher or research sponsor are met. Check the page numbers, the labelling, the tedious nature of the references. Does everyone in your submission appear in your reference list? Are there people in your reference list that do not appear in your submission? The marking criteria may even suggest that a certain percentage of the final mark is awarded for grammar, syntax and spelling, and for the use of referencing but even so, your marker will be human. First impressions may count depending on how that work is read – this should be in a positive way.

The common things to check are: spelling and grammar, punctuation (shorter sentences are preferable), sentence structure, formatting (especially on an electronic screen), references (be aware that potentially your readers may have either written some of the references or know those who have written them), and consistency in the application of terms used throughout. Try not to write 'too academically' – write naturally and use words that you are accustomed to. For example, there is no need to use artificially floral or inventive vocabulary. You will need your personal 'authorial' voice to come through in the text – this is your authenticity as a writer and should be naturally expressed; therefore, allow the proofreading to polish your voice.

How Should You Engage With Proofreading?

The obvious starting point is to allow yourself time and quiet to concentrate. In our experience as dissertation supervisors, we have noted on too many occasions where students have given little time for proofreading, drafting and editing. There has often been ample time for reading, data collection, data analysis, and writing but insufficient time for proofreading. At the outset of your research project, divide time appropriately to ensure that proofreading, and the need for subsequent redrafting, is available. We would suggest that perhaps, a minimum of two weeks could be set aside for this.

Try not to rely too heavily on the spellcheck function on your computer. This could apply to all words, and it may spell words it thinks are correct when you have intended another meaning for them. Yes, the various squiggles and underlines are helpful but only as a starting point. It is a good idea to read paragraphs out of order when proofreading; this is because your brain gets tired quickly and can process information carelessly to save energy. This can result in the brain overlooking errors to create meaning that makes sense to you (recall the double use of 'the' earlier). Some applications have a function whereby the text can be read aloud and this is indeed useful – a good tip is to follow the words on your screen with your finger or pointer.

If you choose to ask others to proofread your work, that is not academic misconduct. Anyone you trust can be a proofreader, but we would advise you to avoid fellow students who are engaged in the same research project module as you. We say this because we have known cases of plagiarism where students have had their work copied, leaving both students liable to accusations of plagiarism. That is a very awkward conversation when both students are in the plagiarism panel together, with only one of them knowing why they are there. Getting a third party to proofread your work is not in itself plagiarism, but you do need to be very careful of letting fellow students have sight of your finished project. There are professional companies, but they can be expensive, and the quality can be varied. Some proofreading opportunities exist with academic support from the university and these will be free. You could ask a family member, friend (who is not connected to your programme of study) or a neighbour, and if you do, suggest a timeline. You need to give them time to read it, to send it back to you, before you are able to give time to edit and redraft. Then there could be the likelihood that you will need to repeat the process.

As a minimum your proofreading should be looking at four areas: spelling and grammar; punctuation; formatting, and referencing, and we look at each of these in turn.

Spelling and Grammar

The list of possible grammar errors that it is possible for any of us to make is long, and some errors (for example the Oxford comma) are even contested, but one of the most common grammar mistakes that students make involves the plural/singular non-agreement of nouns and verbs. For example, phrases such as 'Braun & Clarke (2006) suggests…' should read 'Braun & Clarke (2006) suggest…'. It is true that Braun and Clark wrote that one book, but there are two of them, so the verb needs to reflect plurality.

Other advice we would give in response to common weak features of writing or style are:

- Avoid the use of 'You/we/your', for example '… it is important to have adequate space between tables in your classroom'. The use of 'your' is conversational, it speaks of one very specific classroom, and infers that that one classroom is your reader's.
- Avoid contractions (don't, can't, didn't). Again, this is a conversational style.
- It is useful to use signposting such as subheadings, which help your reader to access and navigate your work.
- Numbers fewer than 100 should be written as words (except for percentages and names such as Year 2 or Key Stage 4).
- Explain all terms first, then abbreviate on subsequent use (English as an additional language – EAL).

- Avoid writing 'research has found' or 'some studies'. Name them at the outset.
- Avoid writing 'I believe' or 'in my opinion'.
- Check your spellchecker, for example, allowing American spellings e.g. behavior.
- Do you know the difference between 'who and whom', 'should of and should have', 'due to and owing to', 'me and my class/my class and me?'
- Look at getting non-sexist terminology and pronouns correct. For example, 'humanity' instead of 'mankind'.

Punctuation

The correct use of full stops, commas, apostrophes, and quotation marks are important in academic writing in a way that have become less so in general writing. In WhatsApp usage, a lot of people correct the punctuation but equally many do not. Across any given student body, this approach to punctuation in general life has inevitably crept into academic writing, and continues to do so. Apostrophes in particular trip up many students. In academic writing an apostrophe will mainly be used for possession, but plural and singular use is different. For example, it is important to know the placing of the apostrophes in the dog's water bowl (one dog); and the dogs' water bowl (more than one dog).

Formatting

It is highly suspicious when the formatting of a submission changes. When the font or font size changes, or line spacing alters, this strongly suggests cutting and pasting. Equally it is very odd if a student is using subheading numbers for most of the submission, and then this stops. You must ensure that all headings, type, font and line spacing follow the guidance provided by your institution, and you are consistent throughout your project. For example, all tables and figures are labelled correctly, then announced in the contents page (Tip: if it is not a table, then it is a figure!). It is essential in a submission the size of a research project to include page numbers, but it would be a rookie error if your page numbers do not match the contents page.

Referencing

This book is not a technical 'How-to-reference' book. Your institution's library will have any number of help guides. You will not lose many marks for an untidy bibliography or reference list, but you will for an incomplete one or one that is poorly ordered. It is also rather unimpressive if a high proportion of your references are websites. Try to cite sources and people, not websites. For example, if you are citing the national curriculum, you should cite DfE (2013) *The national curriculum in England. Framework document for key stages 1 to 4.* Crown copyright, not the generic gov.uk website you may have found it on. All your claims or arguments must be substantiated with a reference or references, and all references in the text must be listed in the reference list, using the referencing system advocated by your university, publisher or sponsor. For example, you might prefer the use of footnotes, and may have successfully used these in another institution, but if your current institution requires the Harvard referencing system, that is what you must do. Harvard does not use footnotes, so neither must you, even if that is your preference. Do not deliberately flout the dress code. That will lose you friends, and marks.

If you cite a reference, it will be assumed that you have read it. Do not apply citations to bulk out your text to try to make your writing look artificially academic. Your writing itself will demonstrate your understanding to your marker, not the number of references. Indeed, the opposite is often true – the way you apply and synthesise sources will show your understanding of your subject far more effectively than the listing of any number of citations. For example, one of the most commonly-cited seminal sources is Vygotsky (1978) from which students name and give a brief description of the famous Zone of Proximal Development model (ZPD). The extent to which students understand this model soon becomes apparent to a marker not from the number of sources they cite to explain it, but through the way in which they apply this model to their project (or misapply it, or sometimes they just name the model, and don't apply it at all). Madison is a case in point. She cited Vygotsky's Zone of Proximal Development in an ill-thought-through attempt to apply some literature to a school's decision to target Learning Assistant support to an area of mathematics under-achievement identified amongst a significant minority of Year 2 children. In the hands of Madison, the ZPD became a teaching and resource strategy designed firstly to benefit a targeted cohort of children in their understanding of a pre-selected maths concept, and secondly to enhance a school's end of Key Stage 1 progress outcome data. Madison would have been better not to have mentioned Vygotsky at all, rather than misapply the ZPD model in such a crass and misinformed way. Her grade tumbled during this oh-so-weak element of her literature review and data analysis.

It is therefore preferable not to cite a source or a theoretical principle unless you are sure of its context. Please do not make the mistake of thinking that when it comes to references, more is better. A small number of well-chosen, well-explained, and effectively contextualised citations is far better than a poorly selected conveyer belt of names and dates.

SUMMARY

The big messages we hope you have taken from this chapter are:

- The time you must spend on your research project is not very near its end once you have written your literature review, methodology and data analysis. The finish line is in sight, but you are not there yet, and the final run-in is uphill. There is still a lot of thought and activity to be done.
- Your conclusion, introduction and abstract should not be seen as a bolt-on. They are integral parts of your research project and will affect your grade just as much as the other chapters. Be sure to give them as much thought.
- Your conclusion, introduction and abstract will probably be written in that order.
- When it comes to referencing, more is not necessarily better.

FURTHER READING

Shields, M. (2010). *Essay writing: A student's guide.* London: SAGE
This book identifies how to cite the range of sources you are most likely to use in your research project.

Vygotsky, L.S. (1978). *Mind in society: The development of higher psychological processes.*
     London: Harvard University Press
This book is a collection of Vygotsky's work, which includes a chapter on the seminal Zone of Proximal Development. It also explores Vygotsky's models of internal mental processes and the foundations of social constructivism. It is not an easy read, but Vygotsky's ideas remain influential.

REFERENCES

Braun, V., & Clarke, V. (2006). Using thematic analysis in psychology. *Qualitative Research in Psychology, 3*(2), 77–101. https://doi.org/10.1191/1478088706qp063oa

DfE. (2013). *The national curriculum in England. Framework document for key stages 1 to 4.* Crown Copyright.

Morgan, R. (2019). 'The practice of the deployment of teaching assistants by trainee teachers during classroom teaching experiences: an issue of negotiation', *Primary First,* (26), pp. 18–25.

Vygotsky, L. S. (1978). *Mind in society: The development of higher psychological processes.* Cambridge MA: Harvard University Press.

12

DISSEMINATION

■■■■■■■■■■■ Chapter Aims ■■■■■■■■■■■

This chapter will explore:

- The need to disseminate your research.
- Ways to disseminate and understanding your intended audience including use of social media.
- Ethical considerations in dissemination.
- Celebrating your research.

THE NEED TO DISSEMINATE YOUR RESEARCH

It is very common for students to experience a sense of anti-climax on submitting their research projects. You have put in all that work, and then it all comes to a shuddering stop, and if you are not careful all that discovery gets locked in a box called Turnitin, or similar, and your findings never see the light of day again. Perhaps your own future professional practice might be influenced by your research, but often it does not go any further than that. It is a shame if that is the case (and it often is), but it does not have to be like this.

You may feel that no one else would be interested in your small-scale project, but there you would be wrong. For one thing, the people who facilitated your project: the participants, the headteacher who gave you permission to undertake the research in their school in the first place, fellow students, all these people would surely have at least a passing professional interest in your work, and some will actively want to know your outcomes and how they might apply to your practice, or theirs. Please do not feel any degree of imposter syndrome or false modesty about your research project. Professional people are interested in the ideas of other professional people. That does not change just because you are new to the profession. The opposite is true. Teachers are interested in fresh ideas, particularly if they are evidence-based and centred on their own school. Of course they would be interested in your work, if only you would have the confidence to tell them about it.

So once you have written your research project, we strongly encourage you to seek a public audience. Dissemination comes from the Latin 'dis + seminare', which means to sow seeds (hence a seminar, and a seminal piece of research). Therefore, it is important that this stage of your work is constructed carefully and without flaws ready for distribution. You would want your findings not only to be read but to receive acknowledgement that they have credence, that someone or an organisation will want to use it to further professional knowledge.

At one level the obvious dissemination point will be your supervisor and the submission centre in your university. You will be submitting a research project or dissertation to attain a grade as part of a wider degree. Even there you will need to ensure that your findings are secure, your methodology and literature reviews are academically expressed and that the outcomes are logical. If you are very aware of the marking criteria (and you would be amazed how few students refer to these) and ensure all are satisfied, this will help to ensure that the opportunity for dissemination is at least plausible.

Some students may feel, with some degree of finality, that the act of submitting their research project is enough. The research ends there. We respect that decision, but this chapter is written for those students who want to take their findings further. For example, if you have written about the development of boys' reading for pleasure, it would make sense to at least utilise the findings in your classroom practice in your first teaching post, but how much better it would be to bring your work into the public domain for the benefit of others.

UNDERSTANDING YOUR AUDIENCE

Your research was written for a particular purpose, not only because it was of interest to you or to other people, but maybe it also addressed a problem or a confusion. This means that your work could affect others – your teaching team, wider colleagues or be useful to a small CPD event. Your findings could improve classroom practice, influence school policy or be an instigator for reform. You should not underestimate the importance of your research – while it may not be earth shattering, it will still have meaning and relevance. Filling a niche is as important as bridging a chasm. Remember that with good supervision, appropriate ethical clearance and sound methodology that the research has a purpose and therefore it is legitimate in contributing to a wider academic community; it is adding to collective knowledge and received wisdom and professional practice. This means it is developing professional growth.

In your ethics section you may have promised that the participants' reward for volunteering their thoughts and time during the data collection period would be to be in receipt of the final project or a summary of it. Therefore, from an ethical point of view it is right to share these outcomes with the participants who would also benefit from collated research. Dissemination also goes further than self-development and from immediate colleagues and research participants. Raising public awareness is arguably why research exists at all – think of medicine for example. Public good can be achieved by sharing your research, and in social media (covered later in this chapter) can be a very efficient way of doing so. In this way the research cycle can be said to close because what is the point of research unless it is communicated to others?

WAYS TO DISSEMINATE

If you are reading this far, you have decided to disseminate, and not to be selfish with your research. Good. In disseminating your findings, you are also putting yourself in a position to be an authority on the subject. This is not in a big-headed way, but again, if the methodology is secure and the academic methods are followed, then the outcomes are valid and reliable. You should be confident in communicating your work to others who show an interest. Presenting at a staff meeting, a local authority or multi-academy training session or wider collaboration with a journal, podcast or further study can enhance your credibility as a researcher as well as your CV.

Here is a summary of why you should disseminate:

1 You are influencing improved classroom practice.
2 You are contributing to existing professional development.
3 You may be informing school policy.
4 You are being recognised as a researcher.
5 You are contributing ethically to the public good.
6 It looks good on your CV.

The starting point is the implementation of your research in your own practice, for example, in your classroom so the immediate recipients of the research will benefit. That will ripple out to colleagues and wider professional contacts, becoming increasingly public facing. To keep the ripple effect analogy your dissemination could proceed thus:

Local level

- At your school or workplace.
- Within your university.

Mid-level

- Academic sharing platforms.
- Local authority events.

Wider level

- Publications.
- Conferences.
- Professional networks.

Social media

- Personal promotion.
- Organisational promotion.

Here is an example of what this could look like as dissemination in practice, at a local level, moving to a mid-level model, then to a wider level:

Temitope, a final-year BA Primary Education QTS student, wrote a dissertation on *the impact of outdoor learning on primary pupils' engagement in English lessons*. She collected the data for this during her final teaching placement.

After completing her project, Temitope:

1 Shared a summary of her findings with her placement school, highlighting practical activities that improved engagement.
2 Presented her work at the university's student research conference using a poster, which drew interest from a local headteacher.
3 Delivered a 20-minute CPD session for staff at her placement school during an INSET day, using real pupil quotes (with permission) and examples of lesson plans.
4 Uploaded her dissertation to the university's open-access repository so other teachers could access it.
5 Adapted part of the dissertation into a short article for a practitioner journal with the encouragement of her research supervisor.

It may not be the case that all steps would necessarily happen, but Temitope's experience is an indication of the potential for a nascent researcher such as yourself. Your starting point will be the time available to you to disseminate as widely as possible, either by you creating the time, or being given time by your employer or research sponsor. But the important thing to remember is to disseminate regardless of the level of audience. There will be others who will be interested to read what you have researched and may want to implement aspects of it, therefore, please have the confidence to disseminate. Your research will have merit and that will be your inspiration.

To disseminate further you will need to a) understand the audience, b) understand what is required and c) know when the deadlines are. Table 12.1 is an indication of what could be disseminated.

USE OF SOCIAL MEDIA

The academic world has shifted online, and it is in this sphere where you could be making an efficient impact. You may want to consider building your research profile in a private capacity or aligned to a professional organisation. Privately this may involve creating a LinkedIn profile, an Instagram or TikTok account, ensuring that they should be separate (and new) accounts to any existing ones you have in a social capacity. It would be encouraged that you join a professional or subject-based association, or a research community. Their ready-made platforms would enable you to contribute.

It is key though, that you develop your profile, contribute in a thoroughly professional manner so your profile is visible and trusted. Consider confidentiality online, check the rules of the hoisting platform, acknowledge sources that are not your own, use appropriate language and engage respectfully.

Table 12.1 The Dissemination Plan

Audience	Platform	What to Disseminate	When to Disseminate	Next Steps
School colleagues (during placement)	School intranet/email	Summary of practice	When approved by placement mentor or headteacher	Ask for feedback
School colleagues (when qualified)	Own practice Staff meeting INSET	Practical suggestions	When signified by headteacher in planning	Ask for feedback – ask for monitoring
At university	University research repository	Dissertation with abstract	When graded and passed by university examination board	See if university has its own publication
Academic sharing events	Those with ORCID or ResearchGate etc.	Abstract and link to abstract (Abstract determines whether it is wanted)	Usually, the next term after originally submitted at university	Create Research profile e.g. ORCID
Local authority events and CPD	Local authority websites	Poster	In first year of qualifying as a teacher	Reach out to wider professional networks
Conferences	Attend in person	Poster Summary of key points	In first year of qualifying as a teacher	Attend yearly and branch out to wider, more prestigious organisations
Professional publications	Their platforms e.g. websites, blogs, video platforms	Abstract and a lengthy summary of dissertation	In first year of qualifying as a teacher	Join accredited network
Social media	Various Podcasting LinkedIn, Bluesky, TikTok, Instagram TED	Variety of dissemination lengths and types dependent on the platform	When graded and passed by university examination board	Keep updating content, look for new social media platforms

Source: Created using a prompt response from ChatGPT; subsequently adapted and edited for accuracy.

You may want to develop your academic profile using platforms such as LinkedIn, YouTube, Vimeo, The Conversation UK or BrightTALK. Table 12.2 shows how some of the current platforms can be used dependent on what and how you wish to disseminate (and, yes, as we have been suggesting, we acknowledge how AI helped us create this table). One obvious point is that newer platforms will appear, and you will need to judge their efficacy.

Table 12.2 Online Dissemination Platforms

Platform	Type	Why Use It as a Beginner?	Strengths	Things to Know
LinkedIn	Professional networking	Share achievements, connect with teachers, mentors, or professional bodies.	Large professional audience, integrates with CV.	Posts should be professional; free version is sufficient.
ResearchGate	Academic network	Share your first research paper, see how peers communicate.	Focused on research, shows downloads and citations.	Mostly used by academics; requires a published piece to upload.
Academia.edu	Academic network	Easy way to showcase your dissertation.	Searchable by topic, beginner-friendly.	Some features may need paid plan.
ORCID	Research ID/ profile	Create a verified researcher profile for future publications.	Permanent ID links to publications.	Doesn't act like social media.
Mendeley	Reference manager and social	Build a personal library and join groups in your field.	Organises references, discover papers.	Networking is smaller; best used alongside research management.
Bluesky	Decentralised microblogging	Share short updates, research ideas, or interesting findings.	Curated communities, more thoughtful discussion.	Smaller audience than mainstream social media.
TED	Talks/events	Inspire others with research ideas.	Global reach, credible platform.	Usually requires application or invitation.
PechaKucha	Presentation format	Practice presenting research in 6–7 minutes.	Creative storytelling, engaging format.	Short, strict timing for slides.

Table 12.2 Online Dissemination Platforms *(Continued)*

Platform	Type	Why Use It as a Beginner?	Strengths	Things to Know
Ignite Talks	Presentation format	Quick way to summarise research findings.	Fast-paced, eye-catching.	Limited to 5-minute talks.
YouTube	Video sharing	Share recorded presentations or explainers.	Massive audience, visual storytelling.	Requires recording/editing effort.
SlideShare	Presentation sharing	Upload slides, posters, or research summaries.	Easy to access, shareable.	Interaction is limited; best for reference materials.
Figshare	Open research repository	Make your dissertation outputs publicly available.	Assigns a DOI for citation.	Mainly academic audience; free account available.
The Conversation UK	Article platform	Write for a general audience about your research.	Media reach, improves communication skills.	Articles are edited before publication.

Source: Created using a prompt response from ChatGPT; subsequently adapted and edited for accuracy.

When disseminating online, do be careful about your online profile. You need to create a professional image. Try not to cross post from your non-professional social media accounts – keep the content related to the area of expertise or discussion. Please be mindful of the replies that come back, not everyone is going to agree with you but with careful curation of your content and platform a professional dialogue about your research question, methods and outcomes can be managed.

Here are some examples of how to approach relevant organisations to disseminate your research:

Ceyda wrote this email to the deputy head of her school placement.

━━━━━ **Ceyda's Email** ━━━━━

Subject: Sharing Research on Outdoor Learning and Literacy Engagement

Dear Colin,

I am writing to share the outcomes of my recently completed dissertation, which explores the impact of outdoor learning on primary pupils' engagement in literacy lessons. My study contains findings which you may mind interesting and may be relevant to the school's ongoing plan for CPD activities or teaching strategies.

(Continued)

Please find attached a summary, and the full dissertation is available via this link [insert link]. I would be happy to have the opportunity to discuss the research or offer a brief presentation to you or at a staff meeting if this would be of interest.

Thank you again for the support provided throughout my placement, and in enabling me to undertake this research project.

Kind regards,
Ceyda

Seren wrote this email to a UK national subject based association.

■■■■■■■■■■ Seren's Email ■■■■■■■■■■

Dear Dr Butler,

My name is Seren, and I am a final-year undergraduate student at [University Name], currently completing my degree in Primary Education. I have recently completed a research project titled "To what extent can therapy dogs contribute to the ethos of a school' that explores teachers' perceptions of how therapy dogs can help to calm or motivate children in Key Stage 2.

Given the focus of your association on broad aspects of primary education, I hope my findings may be of interest to your members and could contribute to ongoing professional discussions. I would welcome the opportunity to share a summary of my research or to contribute a blog post, article, or presentation for your newsletter, website, or upcoming events.

Please let me know if this would be of interest or if there are any specific guidelines I should follow. I appreciate your time and consideration and look forward to your response.

Kind regards,
Seren [surname]
[University]
[Contact Information]

To understand your audience, you will need to do your research. Begin by considering who will benefit from receiving your research. This will be easy at school level but with careful preparation you will be able to select the audience, for example, TAs, parents, subject leaders, or middle management. Trawl professional websites, blogs, vlogs, podcasts, social media outlets, journals selectively. You may want to use search terms to save you wandering off track. For example, BERA or the National Association of Primary Education (NAPE) may be calling for article writers. Temper your pitch and your presentation (see Table 12.1) as to how you might use language or a presentation format. Such organisations will also have clear guidance of how articles can be submitted (and usually rejected if not followed). Join a professional network, for example the History Association and keep up to date in the field.

Although it is exciting to build your research or academic profile, online or in print, it is important to do two things. First, is to track where you have submitted your research and to track its impact. This is important in building a CV, or for career development. Second, it is important not to be despondent with rejection. This does happen a lot, but being rejected comes with many reasons and is normally accompanied by appropriate and helpful feedback. Act on this for the next time.

ETHICAL CONSIDERATIONS IN DISSEMINATION

Before you do disseminate it is important to be mindful of the ethics involved. Your project with its anonymously collected data is now entering the public sphere. This means that all those ethical issues you considered prior to the data collection will now need to be recalled. Check again that you have all the signed consent letters so that the published data within the final research project is accounted for. In other words, all data that is published must not be able to be traced to the participants, so you must ensure that all people and institutions are anonymised or given pseudonyms, and all participants have given their assent or consent for you to publish in this way. For example, you must go through your emails and check that no-one has decided to withdraw their permission to the data. This should be done regularly, but although rare, it could happen. If it does, you will have to delete the data and amend your findings.

In your dissemination, and certainly in the data analysis and conclusion chapters, only claim that which is valid. Do not make a claim for something that is not correct or exaggerated. This is not helpful; to you, the research participants or to the academic community. If you agreed to something during the research, then please ensure you uphold it. This can range from agreeing to give the head teacher the research project on completion, or to submit it somewhere, or not to submit it somewhere.

Giving your research participants an early copy of your research project is a reward for them in participating – so they will feel they got something out of the process. If participants feel they have been treated well, notably from an ethical position, as well as from courteous research, then they will be more likely to contribute to future research with yourself or others. The academic community relies on high standards, ethical researchers, and willing volunteers.

Finally, in your dissemination you may want to give ethical considerations to social justice, reducing discrimination, paper consumption and how modern technology, for example the use of AI and data centres, have an impact on water usage.

CELEBRATING YOUR RESEARCH

Well done! You have got this far, and you should be proud of your achievements. Now you have completed a successful piece of research you are inducted by right into the wider academic community. You can now see yourself as a researcher and that identity is important because it will now be assumed that you continue developing, maturing as an academic researcher.

You will recall above that we wrote about the need to have a polished final submission. Even though on submitting your research project you may feel that you never want to look at it again, it may turn out that after a while (typically about a year) you may re-read your submission and think *'Oh that could be improved'* or *'I wish I had included/deleted that'*. Such thoughts are understandable and are the sign of how much you have moved on. That is why academic research does not stop, you keep going, by researching more in depth or something else, but crucially, acquiring more, better and deeper skills.

Celebrate your achievements on passing your initial research project, and then start to build your research portfolio, update your CV to include your research interests (this is a very strong thing to do on a CV), and find your research niche and expertise. You could find someone willing to be your research mentor, maybe your former university supervisor, or someone from your employer network or from a professional association. Now that you are in the academic research community, keep learning, asking questions, and above all enjoy researching. You have earned the right to be there, and to identify as a researcher.

FURTHER READING

Bell, J., Waters, S. and Johnson, H. (2024). *Doing your research project*. 8th edn. Maidenhead: OUP/McGraw Hill. See Chapter 16, writing the report.
An easy-to-read textbook, written in a student-friendly style that uses reflective questions to guide the student through their research project.

Robson, C. (2024). *Real world research*. 5th edn. Chichester: John Wiley & Sons Ltd. See Chapter 19, Reporting, disseminating and moving forward.
A thorough textbook regarding research, that is easy to read and full of appropriate examples for a first-time researcher.

INDEX